GW01007514

TUNING ANGLIAS & CORTINAS
including the classic
capri V4 and twin cam

speedsport

1st Impression September 1969
2nd Impression May 1970
3rd Impression August 1970
4th Impression November 1973

Large parts of this book first appeared
in 1967 as Tuning Small Fords

ISBN 0-85113-003-8

© Speedsport Motobooks 1973

Published by
Speedsport Motobooks
Bercourt House, York Road, Brentford,
Middlesex, TW8 0QP, England.

Printed in Great Britain by
HGA Printing Company Limited
Brentford, Middlesex

CONTENTS

CHAPTER 1
birth of the breed

Fords' first Anglia was announced in October, 1939. Twenty years later, the "new Anglia" was announced, with its advanced 105E series power unit— oversquare cylinder dimensions, over-head valves, and mated to a four-speed gearbox, to say nothing of an unusual body style. This car really started some-thing, to put it mildly. The new car was introduced in September, 1959, and as part of the introduction publicity two models were used as course cars at a BRSCC race meeting at Brands Hatch. The main race of the day was an event for the then-new Formula Junior; by the end of the following season the 105E engine, tuned by Cosworth and mounted in the Lotus 18, was completely domin-ating the Formula, as it then continued to do throughout. Since then, engines of the 105E family have been leading in motoring competition of all kinds, and have been extensively tuned and mod-ified for road and competition use.

The 105E Anglia, with its 997 c.c., o.h.v. engine (bore and stroke 80.97 mm x 48.41 mm, 39 b.h.p. at 5,000 r.p.m.) continued virtually unchanged until the model was discontinued, to be re-placed by the Escort, in November,

1967. Estate car and van versions were introduced in August and June, 1961, respectively, and in October, 1959, a month after the Anglia's announce-ment, the 107E Prefect joined the range. This featured the 195E engine and gear-box mounted in the square-rigged 100E Anglia/Prefect shell (this model, with the 1172 c.c. side-valve engine had been the Ford small car range from 1953-59). Unlike the Anglia, the Prefect version had a short life, and was withdrawn from the range in May, 1961.

Meanwhile, the next development in the new range was ready. This was the 1340 c.c. 109E, with an unchanged bore of 80.97 mm but a new stroke of 65.07 mm. With a compression ratio of 8.5 to 1, maximum power was 54 b.h.p. at 4,900 r.p.m. This engine was first fitted in the Classic 315, introduced in May, 1961; in January, 1962, it found its way into the two-seater Capri, a long-tailed "personal" car which, of course, has no connection with the current bearer of the name.

The 109E 1340 c.c. engine was cont-inued until August ,1962, being replaced in the Classic and Capri by the next development, the 116E engine. Still with a bore of 80.97 mm, this had a still longer stroke of 72.74 mm, still retaining the oversquare characteristics and, with a compression ratio of 8.3 to 1, developing 59.5 b.h.p. at 4.600 r.p.m. from its 1498 c.c.

A month later, Ford introduced another new car—the Cortina, in September, 1962. The power unit for this car was to be yet another derivative of the 105E family—the 113E, with a capacity of 1198 c.c. from the same 80.97 mm bore and a stroke of 58.17 mm. With an initial compression ratio of 8.7 to 1, maximum power was 48.5 b.h.p. at 4,800. In October, 1962, this engine was fitted to the Anglias—the 997 c.c. version remained in the range—and the model was designated the Anglia Super, and in October, 1964, the compression ratio was raised to 9.1 to 1, resulting in an increase in maximum power to 50 b.h.p. at 4,900 r.p.m.

In January, 1963, the 118E Cortina was announced—the new medium-sized car now fitted with the 1498 c.c. engine. Estate car versions of the Cortina, with both 1198 and 1498 c.c. engines, came in March, 1963 and in April there came the Cortina GT, with a more highly-tuned version of the 116E engine which had been available on the Capri since February, 1963. This had changes in carburation, manifolding and an increase in compression ratio to 9 to 1, to give an increased power output of 78 b.h.p. at 5,200 r.p.m'

In October, 1963 the Classic was dropped, and the Corsair range introduced, with the 1500 and 1500 GT engines already available in the Cortina and Capri and the sharp-nosed body-style which is, of course, retained in the current V4 range.

The same year saw the introduction of yet another variation of the engine—the 125E, which has since become one of the most successful and popular competition engines ever produced. This was the Lotus variation of the Cortina GT engine, with twin-overhead camshafts and a power output of 105 b.h.p. at 5,500 r.p.m. Compression ratio was up to 9.5 to 1, there were two twin-choke Weber carbs and, alone of the range so far, the bore was different, being enlarged to 82.55 mm. With a normal 1498 c.c. engine stroke of 72.74 mm, this gave a capacity of 1558 c.c. and the engine was fitted in the first of the Lotus-Cortina range, basically a two-door Cortina shell with lower, stiffer front suspension and a completely redesigned rear end employing coil springs, trailing links and "A" brackets. This continued until late 1965, when the rear suspension reverted to normal Cortina-type, but the cars lost a lot of their original "hard" character with the change, which also involved a change to lower intermediate gearing, a softer ride and greater reliability.

In September, 1966 the existing range of Cortinas was dropped, to be replaced by the Mark II versions with restyled bodywork and new engines. The old three-bearing crank, 1198 c.c. engine was replaced by a new 1300: the same bore of 80.97 mm was retained, but a new stroke measurement of 62.99 mm gave a capacity of 1297 c.c.; the new engine had the five-bearing crankshaft of the 1498 c.c. range and with a compression ratio of 9 to 1 maximum power was 57.5 b.h.p. at 5,000 r.p.m. A new 1500 engine also retained the 80.97 mm bore, but a marginally longer stroke of 72.82 mm (instead of 72.74 mm) gave a capacity of 1499 c.c. With 9 to 1 compression ratio in normal form, maximum power was 65 b.h.p. at 4,750 r.p.m. (an increase of 6 b.h.p.). A GT version of the new engine, with Weber carb, new manifolding and larger inlet valves provided maximum power of 83.5 b.h.p. at 5,200 r.p.m., with a significant increase in torque. The GT version was available with $4\frac{1}{4}$ in. section rims as an optional extra, and all the Mk. II versions were fitted with four-speed, all-synchromesh gearboxes and diaphragm-spring clutches.

These were only "interim" engines; in September, 1967 Ford introduced the first of the now-complete range of cross-flow engines for the Cortina. These came in 1300, 1600 and 1600 GT types, with the addition of a newcomer to the Cortina range, the 1600E. This combined a rather more de luxe interior trim with Cortina-Lotus suspension and 1600GT power unit. The engines themselves were fundamentally similar to the revised 1300 and 1500 units of the previous year, but with obvious differences. The 1300 retained the same bore and stroke (80.97 mm x 62.99 mm) with a crossflow cylinder head, new pistons incorporating the combustion chambers, revised manifolding to match the cross-flow port layout and different settings for the Autolite carb. On the 1600, however, there was, in addition, a capacity change: bore remained the same old 80.97 mm, but the stroke was increased to 77.62 mm to give a capacity of 1599 c.c. With a 9 to 1 compression ratio, power output was 58 b.h.p. at 5,000 r.p.m. (unchanged to all intents and purposes) for the 1300, 71 b.h.p. at 5,000 r.p.m. for the normal 1600 and 88 b.h.p. at 5,400 r.p.m. for the Weber-equipped 1600 GT. Engine mounting-points, camshaft and overall dimensions were the same as on the 1500/1300 models, and head, pistons and so on apart, the only other item of significant difference was the starter motor, which was not interchangeable with that used on previous models.

The only other variation among power units on the Anglia-Cortina-Corsair range dealt with in this book was the introduction of the V4 engines, fitted to the Corsair in September, 1965. Two differing engines were employed, according to whether your Corsair was a normal type or a GT. In the former case, the power unit fitted was a 1663 c.c. version, designated the 1700: bore and stroke were 93.66 mm x 60.35 mm, giving 84 b.h.p. at 4,750 r.p.m. on a 9 to 1 compression ratio. The GT was given a 2-litre engine, with a same bore as the smaller version but with a longer (72.4 mm) stroke to give a total capacity of 1996 c.c. A compression ratio of 8.9 to 1 helped to produce a maximum of 97 b.h.p. at 4,750, and at the same time the car was given a heftier clutch (8 in. instead of 7.5. in.) and much closer gear ratios in the four-speed, all-synchromesh box. During 1966 a Corsair estate car, based on 2-litre GT mechanical components, was introduced, while for 1968 the GT Corsair became the Corsair 2000E, with improved interior trim, wider $4\frac{1}{2}$ in. wheels, carburation and manifolding which made a smoother and more powerful car.

Ignoring, for a moment, the V4 engines and the odd variations which have already been mentioned, all the engines in this range share similar characteristics and the principal differences between them lie in the stroke, con-rod centres, crankshafts, cam lift and valve sizes: as already mentioned, it will be obvious that the twin-cam and crossflow engines also employ completely different pistons and cylinder heads. All bores, except where stated, are constant at 80.97 mm. Cam lift on all engines other than GT versions and the twin-cam and V4 range is 0.2108 (inlet) and 0.2176 (exhaust); on GT versions, the lift is 0.2309 (inlet) and 0.2321 (exhaust). All engines, obviously, have varying con-rod centres, from 4.611-4.612 for the 997 to 4.799-4.801 for the 1500. Sump capacity varies for the 1498, 1500 and 1600 models, where capacity is $6\frac{1}{4}$ pints; on all other engines, it is four pints.

Serial No.	Model	c.c.	introduced
105E	Anglia	997	Sept., 1959
107E	Prefect	997	Oct. 1959
	Classic 315		May 1961
109E	Capri 335	1340	Jan., 1962
113E	Cortina	1198	Sept., 1962
	Classic 315		August, 1962
	Classic 315		Aug., 1962
116E	Capri	1498	Aug., 1962
	Capri GT		Feb., 1963
	Cortina-		Jan., 1963
118E	Super	1498	
	Cortina GT		April, 1963
120E	Corsair	1498	Oct., 1963
123E	Anglia	1198	Oct., 1962
	Super		
125E	Cortina-	1558	Oct., 1962
	Lotus		

Four sizes of oversize piston are available for all engines: these are 0.005, 0.015, 0.025 and 0.030. Valve sizes on the 997, 1198 and 1340 engines are identical at 1.262-1.272 (inlet) and 1.183-1.193 (exhaust) head diameter; the 1498 and 1500 engines are 1.432-1.442 (inlet) and 1.183-1.193 (exhaust) and on the 1500 GT engine the diameters are 1.405-1.415 (inlet) and 1.24-1.25 (exhaust). Valve stem diameter, valve guide bore diameter and stem clearance in the guide are identical on all engines.

Three standard final drive ratios are available: 3.9 to 1, 4.125 to 1 and 4.44 to 1, the smaller-engined cars normally having one of the two lower alternatives and the 3.9 normally being fitted only to 1500, 1600, GT and Lotus models. A very wide range of further alternatives is available from the Ford Performance Centre at Boreham, near Chelmsford, Essex.

Carburation has varied considerably. On recent models Autolite carburettors are fitted to normal-engined cars, with Weber instruments on GT models. Earlier cars had Solex carbs fitted to Anglia 997 and 1200 models and the jetting and choke dimensions were revised in May, 1962; 1340 and early 1500 (not GT) models had Zenith VN2 instruments.

CHAPTER 2
principles of tuning

The first thing we have to understand about this range of engines is that the very beginning of worthwhile tuning is in modifications to the cylinder head. Simply bolting on twin S.U.s or a twin-choke carburettor of some sort is to all intents and purposes no good at all, and just about the only result you will notice is that the car will consume a great deal more petrol. On the 1200 engine you might gain an extra 2 b.h.p. but, once again, the engine will drink a disproportionate amount more petrol in terms of the increase in performance. Much the same applies to the 1340 engine.

The 1500 would respond a little better to the fitting of additional carburation, and the gain on this engine might, perhaps, be another 4 b.h.p. over standard.

The reasons for this are, quite simply, in the breathing characteristics of the standard head. That of the 1200 is slightly better than the 997, and the 1340 is almost identical. The 1500 has slightly better ports and valves. All these engines, except the 1500 G.T., use the same camshaft.

The same applies to exhaust manifolds.

With just a four-branch exhaust of however good a design, the improvement in power over the standard job would be roughly the same as you would get by fitting an additional carburettor: both the extra carburation and the four-branch manifold would, again, give only a small improvement which would hardly be justified by the trouble and expense of putting them on. So the obvious thing to do first is to modify the head. On an otherwise standard 997 engine a properly reworked head will give another 5 b.h.p. and, if combined with additional carburation, will give an extra 9 b.h.p. and this applies equally to the 1200 and 1340.

The 1500, oddly enough, with head and carburettor mods will only give another 7 b.h.p. or so, the reason for this being quite simply that the head is more efficient to start with.

If you add a four-branch manifold to this arrangement of head and carbs you can get another 3 b.h.p. for the 997 and 1200, but, once again, practically nothing on the 1500. Because this latter engine is so much better to start with, you have to do much more to it to show any real results. The same sort of results will be gained from the other sort of "instant tune"—fitting the G.T. camshaft in the ordinary 1500 engine. Simply fitting the G.T. cam and keeping the rest of the engine standard is a complete waste of time. Fitting the G.T. head to a 1500 is an expensive pastime and, in any case, you can get better results by modifying the existing head unless you want to bring it up to G.T. specification with larger valves and so on. If you fit the G.T. camshaft, plus head and carburettor mods, to the 997 engine you will get about 66 b.h.p., and about 76 on the 1200 and 1340. On the 1500 you will get about the same as on a standard G.T. 1500 if you add the G.T. exhaust as well—about 78 b.h.p. It's worth mentioning at this point that bringing a 1500 engine up to G.T. power output doesn't by any means make it a G.T. engine—the proper G.T. motor has lead-indium bearings, stronger pistons and a stronger clutch which can be rather important. In fact, if you modify a 1200 to give more than 60 b.h.p. the 109E clutch is advisable.

By now anyone who has gone to all this trouble will also have replaced the exhaust system with something a bit more efficient, but this isn't necessary with power outputs below, say, 55 b.h.p.

Head-Swapping

Head-swapping is another popular pastime among those who try to get more power out of engines of other manufacturers, but while this may produce results in those cases it doesn't make a jot of difference to the small Fords. Fitting, say, a 1200 head on a 997 engine will simply give you a slower car because of the reduced compression ratio—the same applies to the 1500 head, only more so. It is important to bear in mind that the best results will be achieved by modifying the proper head for the engine. When it comes to doing this, bear in mind that the maximum

amount you can safely take off the 105E, 109E, 113E and 116E heads is 80 thous.—this is a safe maximum for the average head. Any more than this and you might run into water passages, or the head might even crack through lack of thickness. If you really want to take off more than this you have to scrounge the local Ford dealers for the best head you can find, and if you chance to find a good enough one it might be possible to take off up to 120 thou. or more off it. This, however, is seldom possible except on a very carefully selected head.

So far as reliability is concerned, you can reckon that driven reasonably and properly maintained, an engine tuned to produce the sort of power we've been talking about up till now will last for about fifty thousand miles before it needs attention. And this sort of power —66 b.h.p., for example, on a 997 engine, will give a maximum speed of 97-98 m.p.h., and about the same on the 1200 and 1340 engines if they are modified to a similar degree. With the larger engine you get less improvement in maximum speed compared with a tuned 997, but obviously you get better acceleration. The principal weakness on the three-bearing crankshaft engines was the centre main-bearing cap, which was subject to failure even on standard engines. This was improved on later models by fitting a slightly different the three-bearing crankshaft engines is the centre main-bearing cap, which are subject to failure even on standard engines. This has been improved on later models by fitting a slightly different cap which has about an extra 100 thou. thickness, but while this helps it doesn't by any means solve the problem and, anyway, as far as existing engines are concerned it doesn't help much since Fords won't sell the thicker caps without the block. The other limiting factors on the three-bearing engines were the rods themselves, while on the five-bearing

Courtesy Ford Motor Company

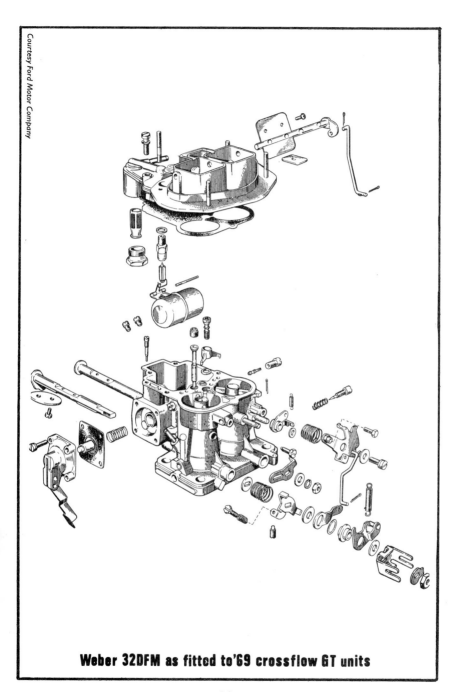

Weber 32DFM as fitted to '69 crossflow GT units

engines it is rods and crankshaft which are most likely to fail. For this reason any engine in the range should be limited to six-five as maximum sustained revs if you are in any way interested in long life, and this is a point to bear in mind if you are thinking of mods which need extra revs to achieve their full effect: for instance, fitting the G.T. camshaft to the 997, when for the extra power it will want to run on for another thousand revs or so before it dies away. The best way round the centre main-bearing shell weakness is to have some special bearing shells made up: I did 40,000 miles in two years on a 1340 with these bearing shells made up. But although the shells can be improved the cap weakness still remains.

Interchangeability

In general terms, all these engines and cars are more or less interchangeable, using the same mountings. However, although it isn't worth spending a fortune on a 997 for road use when for the same money you can fit a 1500 and have a smoother, sweeter and more reliable car, there is an important point to be watched. This is that the cooling systems need to be tweaked—the 1200, for instance, uses a bigger fan than the 997 and this is true of all of them. If you don't do something about this you'll have the thing boiling every time you come to a traffic hold-up, while there is no question of chopping fan blades off or something, which is a big thing with Minis.

So far in this purely general discussion we have only discussed the normal engines, with no reference to the G.T. Cortina at all. The same basic principle applies to this engine as to the others in that for really worthwhile results you must start with the head. A re-worked head, bolted straight on with the same sized valves, will give it another 8 b.h.p.

The next thing to do would be to change the camshaft which will give a good increase in power in the middle range and quite a bit more at the top—up to 102 m.p.h. with a suitable re-jetted carb. But it will put up the tick-over to a very uneven thousand revs, and pulling power won't be too good under 2,000 r.p.m.

Webers

The next step after this is to fit two twin-choke Webers. This will give up to another 9 b.h.p. to make a total output of up to 111, and in addition it will even out the idling and the engine will pull as smoothly as a standard engine from low revs. The trouble—there's always a snag!—is that it will rev far beyond the safe limit of six-five for continuous use on a standard bottom end. The best thing to do is to fit a rev-limiting device in the distributor, which can be set anywhere between six and seven thousand revs. You'll still get the benefit of the power because in this state of tune it will peak at about six thousand.

After this you could increase the valve sizes, but this would lose the bottom-end performance. The best thing to do is to open it up to 1,650 c.c.: this won't mean a colossal increase in actual power, but the torque will be increased very considerable throughout the range. Maximum power will go up by only about 8 b.h.p.

The increase in bore required to bring the engine to 1,650 c.c. is 4 mm., bringing the bore up to 85 mm. And, frankly, the block itself will not necessarily be capable of being bored to this extent—in fact, it is safe to say that the chances against it are at least ninety per cent. The only successful way to do it is to select a block and, of course, while it can be done to any 1500 engine it simply doesn't apply to any of the three-bearing engines.

On the exhaust side, the G.T. Cortina

14

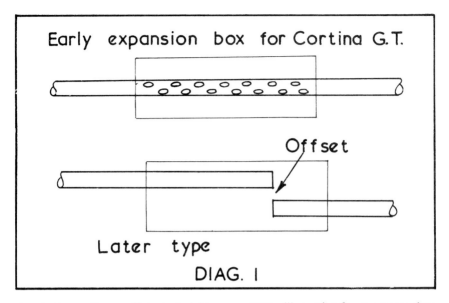

Early expansion box for Cortina G.T.

Offset

Later type

DIAG. I

already has quite an efficient straight-through exhaust system and money spent in this direction doesn't show much improvement. This, however, doesn't apply to the latest models—here a different type of expansion box (see Diag. 1) is used which quite clearly loses power.

All models except the G.T. Cortina and the 1500 are fitted with copper-asbestos head gaskets. The G.T. and 1500 have composition gaskets which can give trouble on planed heads and where the engine is giving more power they are liable to blow. Thus when modifying the 1500 or G.T. head you should fit a normal copper-asbestos gasket as used on the 997, 1200 and 1340.

The same valve springs are fitted to all the latest models, but if in doubt you can fit the 109E springs. These are quite satisfactory for road cars in almost any state of tune, and depending on the camshaft (which can vary from one engine to another in standard form) will allow up to 7,000 r.p.m. before the point of valve-bounce is reached. A 997

or 1200 will permit a few more revs than the 1500 because the valves and push rods are lighter, which is entirely logical, and so for that matter are the pistons.

So far as road cars are concerned, crank-balancing is a bit of a waste of time with a six-five rev-limit, especially as they are already balanced to extraordinarily fine limits at the factory. If you went to Fords and saw this being done it would undoubtedly surprise you! Since the initial manufacture of these engines, the cranks and con-rods have improved a great deal. Crankshafts for the three-bearing engine, for instance, were initially hollow but on late models were solid right through, as well as being much better finished. The 116E crank has been superseded by the 116B which is, again, a marked improvement. Con-rods were improved to a terrific extent after 1964 and have much stronger bolts than early models, although they remain interchangeable, luckily. Small-end and big-end holes, which in the early days **were by no means infrequently offset in** the rod, are now invariably nicely concentric within the forging, but there has been no change in material of crank or rods. In all models all main and big-end bearings are matched by means of paint-codes to the journal, which has helped with the problem of the centre main bearing on three-bearing engines although it hasn't eliminated it. The matching does, however, give an increased life.

Rods should not be polished, and those which are tend to be more liable to crack because a hard skin formed on the outer surface during manufacture is removed by polishing, which weakens the whole rod.

The 1500 engines have very heavy flywheels, but there is no point in attempting to lighten them because you can fit the much lighter component from the 105E engine which both fits and does the job. However, you have to remember that while this will make the engine more responsive to the throttle, it will also make it less pleasant to drive in traffic.

On the electrical side, all distributors are different from model to model, but this shouldn't worry anyone contemplating modifications, because we can get decent petrol in this country, and provided it is in good working order there should be no need to change it. Obviously, for the very best results you should use the right distributor, with the right advance curve, for the model.

Lubrication for small Fords tuned for road use doesn't present any problems. The 1500 has a bigger sump (by a couple of pints) than the others, but Fords in general don't suffer from boiling oil and an oil cooler shouldn't be necessary. If you want to increase the oil pressure, you simply stick a quarter-inch spacer behind the relief valve spring—again, this isn't really necessary. The normal 35 p.s.i., with practically nothing on tickover, is satisfactory—in fact a standard engine should have about 10 p.s.i. on tickover unless the pump is badly worn, and frankly nothing you can do to the pressure relieve valve will alter the idling-speed pressure. Later engines are fitted with a larger-capacity oil filter which takes an extra one-third of a pint of oil, but it confers no practical advantages apart from a longer interval between changes of the (more expensive) filter element.

The easiest way to get more power from a Ford engine is, without a doubt, to fit a bigger one—if you can afford it. The snag is that the biggest and best—the Cortina G.T.—is expensive, and although the price covers clutch, dynamo, water-pump and so on, and while the engine will go straight into an Anglia, it's still a lot of money to find all at one go. But if you can do it, you will end up with a reliable, smooth car with a 100 m.p.h. top speed and a 0-60 time of around 11 seconds. This sort of performance in an Anglia runs you straight into handling and braking problems, of course, but we'll go into that more deeply in a later chapter.

CHAPTER 3
tuning the anglia

Motor-cars are expensive things, and their component parts tend to be proportionately costly, too. So before any tuning work is attempted it is important to work out exactly what you are going to do before going off "half-cocked" and damaging some major component beyond repair so that it must be replaced. This particularly applies to cylinder head work, where it is important to bear in mind that although it is the easiest thing in the world to take metal off it is a good deal more difficult, and often completely impossible, to replace it if we take off too much. So we want to look before we leap and think carefully before we act.

Another point. The car as it comes out of the factory is designed with brakes and suspension to cope with a given performance—the standard performance in fact. Any increase in this performance can mean that the brakes and/or roadholding can become inadequate, and the greater the increase in power we get from the engine the more vital it becomes to make sure that any necessary improvements in these two other departments are made at the same time,

or at least before the car goes back on the road.

This isn't intended to be any kind of workshop manual, so there will be no detailed instructions on how to remove the engine, or replace the valves—I am assuming a basic knowledge of how a car is put together and of what goes on inside it. In the same way reasonable familiarity with workshop tools, and a reasonable stock of equipment, is also assumed, although obviously some of the work, such as head-planing or cylinder block boring will have to be done by professionals in the majority of cases. For any tuning operations you should have a good workshop manual at your elbow.

So far as equipment is needed, Clive Trickey's book on cylinder head modification covers the subject fully and all we need say here is that apart from the usual hammers, mallets, pliers, hacksaws, files and screwdrivers, you need a complete set of best-quality open-ended spanners, and a set of ring-spanners of similar quality. A small socket set is also handy. Then you must have an electric drill—at least 1,400 r.p.m. speed, with a five-sixteenths chuck—and a good flexible shaft. Along with this you want a selection of grinding stones—again the best quality is the cheapest in the long run—of various shapes, in both coarse and fine qualities, and a short rod, slotted to take a strip of abrasive cloth for polishing. A stock of small handfiles of various shapes and sizes more or less completes your basic home tuning kit if you add a rubber disc to which you can attach emery cloth and although this isn't exactly complete it will be enough to make a start and you can add the other shapes and sizes more or less completes your basic home tuning kit if you add a rubber disc to which you can attach emery cloth and although this isn't exactly complete it will be enough to make a start, and you can add the other bits and pieces as you find you need them.

Which brings us back to what we are going to do to the Ford head for tuning for road use. The first step is to remove eighty thou. from it, a straightforward machining job which will nevertheless be beyond the average home workshop, so it will have to be sent away to a machine shop. Taking off this much will send up the compression by a couple of ratios to around, say, 11 to 1 on a 997 head, and if we only want to simply raise the compression ratio only forty thou. need be taken off. However, there's no point in doing half a job and the full eighty thou., which is a safe maximum for the average head, means that we can start work on the chambers. Removing metal from the combustion chambers will obviously have the effect of lowering the compression ratio, but this doesn't matter as the 11 to 1 or so we've achieved as a result of planing the head is far too high—for road use there is no point in going above 10 to 1.

When the head comes back from the machine shop, get a standard, well-compressed but complete and undamaged head gasket and fit it over the head,

lining it up with the bolt-holes and, if necessary, clamping it in place. This will give us the cylinder area, and if we mark this in it will show us how far out we can go. In practice, you can remove about a sixteenth of an inch of metal from round the inlet and exhaust valves, or to put it another way, if we use the valve guide hole as a centre we want to increase the radius of the circle by a sixteenth. For this job you want the electric drill and a selection of grinding stones—the easiest to use for the job the cylindrical shapes. Taking metal off the chambers as we have indicated means that you will be left with a couple of flats at, and opposite, the plug apperture, and these will need blending-in. (See Diag. 2). When you are working inside the chamber with a grinding stone you must be very careful to make sure that there is no possibility of damaging the valve seats, and the easiest way of doing this is to use old valves as blanking pieces which will protect them.

So far as the cross-section shape of the chamber is concerned you must keep the walls vertical, or straight-sided if you prefer it—around the valve so that you get the same area at low valve-lift as at high, but you can afford to put a certain amount of chamfer on as you get to the centre of the chamber where there is no valve.

Having done this you can start polishing, and once you've got the initial polish on —use the abrasive paper discs for this, by the way: it isn't wise to use grinding stones on the roof of the chamber at any time—and taken off all the irregularities you will have to equalise the chambers. For this you need a burette, and the obvious thing to do is to take the volume of the chamber which has worked out as greatest and bring the others up to it. Using the burette, use a mixture of paraffin and oil to find out its volume and when you are enlarging the others to

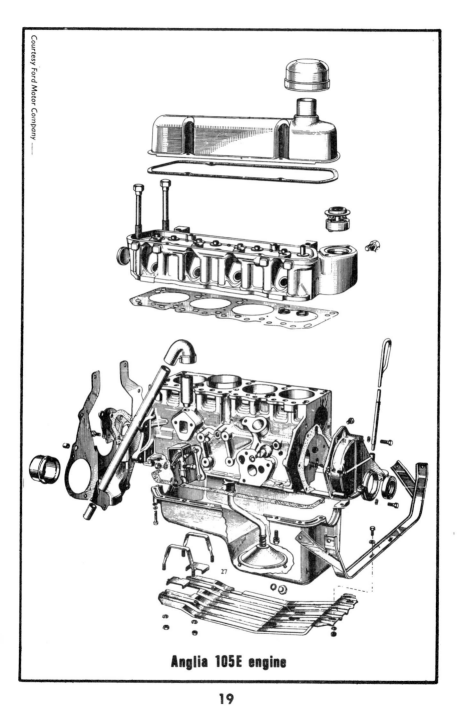

Courtesy Ford Motor Company —

Anglia 105E engine

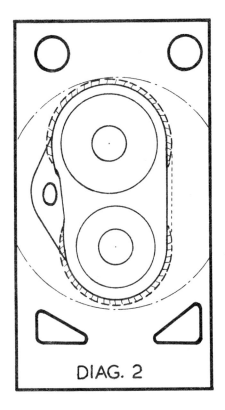

DIAG. 2

match check your work very frequently: as I've already said, you can't put metal back once its off. Under no circumstances "undercut" the gasket area.

When all the chambers are equalised, you can do the final polishing. Care is needed here to see that over-enthusiasm doesn't alter the volume by taking off too much metal from one chamber, and in fact there is no need to bull them up like a mirror—just get a nice smooth finish. Bearing in mind that the conrods will probably all be of different lengths, and that the piston heights will all be different, there is no need to carry this equalising too far, and providing the volumes are equal to, say, a quarter of a c.c. it will be satisfactory.

Stage one tuning

A well-finished head, left as standard with regard to compression ratio but with the combustion chambers balanced, equalised and nicely polished, with the ports matched and polished, can give up to an extra 4 b.h.p. on the 997 c.c. engine and as much as an extra 6 b.h.p. on the 1198. It will also produce a much smoother power unit, and this is definitely the end product, or part of it, to aim at whether you are considering further tuning or not.

In practice, if you are going to do as much work as this on the head you might just as well go in deep on the idea and work out a proper modification programme to give a useful all-round increase in performance. The first step is to remove, or have removed, eighty thou. from the head face, as already indicated, and modify and reshape the chambers as outlined. By the end of all this the compression ratio should be somewhere between 9.5 and 10 to 1, which is as high as is necessary for road use.

The ports are particularly well worth enlarging on the inlet side on both the 997 and 1198 engines: apart from cleaning them up and removing roughness or unnecessary projections, leave the exhaust ports the same dimensions as standard. The inlets will benefit from having about one-sixteenth of an inch of metal removed from the head-face end, and this wants to be worked out so that the amount of metal taken off tapers away to nothing—in other words, standard diameter—at the valve end. Don't alter the shape of the port, but remove the restriction and concentrate on getting a smooth finish for free mixture flow (Diagram 3).

Around the valve-guide hole there is a "step" in the port (Diagram 4) which must not be removed, or the valve guide will be ruined. However, it can—and should—be blended-in gently as shown by the shaded area in the diagram, and

20

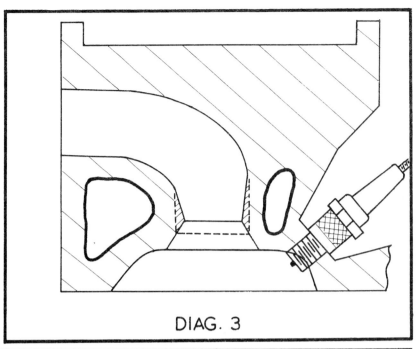

DIAG. 3

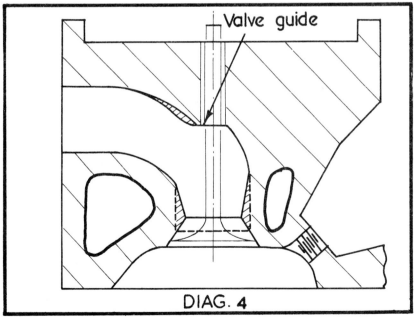

Valve guide

DIAG. 4

With the head modified in this way, the time has come to think about carburation. In fact, immediate results should be beneficial even if the standard set-up is retained, but to do this is simply not getting the full benefit of your labours and to do the job properly it's now time to change. It is impractical to attempt to obtain real benefit by resetting the standard carb. since those fitted to the 997 and 1198 engines have fixed chokes, not adjustable, and although it is possible to enlarge these by a machining operation it isn't really worth the trouble. Alternatively, the mixture can be varied by removing the main jet altogether and replacing it with a larger one, remembering that the air compensating jet will have to be altered at the same time to suit the main jet characteristics. If you really want to make life difficult, it is possible to have the existing choke tube bored out by 2-3 mm, but the limiting factor is the diameter of the butterly, which must obviously not finish up trying to operate satisfactorily in a tube of greater diameter than it is itself.

The best plan is to use a different carburettor altogether. You can fit either the S.U., the Stromberg CD or the 28/36 Weber. In the case of the first two, the $1\frac{1}{4}$ in. S.U. or the 125 CD Stromberg will be adequate for road work, but best results are usually obtained from the 28/36 DCD Weber, which is the instrument fitted as standard to the 1500 G.T. engines. This instrument, if you are going to get the maximum benefit, should be mounted on a good manifold designed to take it—these are widely available from tuning establishments and speed shops—and will naturally need to be re-jetted.

It is absolutely impossible to give a list of settings which will be dead right for all engines, since to a large extent they will be governed by the characteristics of the individual head, and while it may be possible for speed shops to get down

a "standard" range of settings for heads which they have themselves produced and which may be near enough identical, a one-off head such as will have been produced by the home tuner will have characteristics all its own. For the 997/ 1198 engines, however, a reasonable starting point would be as follows in the table:

Chokes	23-25
Main jets	120-130
air correction jets	220-180
emulsion tubes	F30
pilot jets	50-50
pump jets	70

So far as manifolding is concerned, the standard component—an aluminium pressing—is not at all a bad shape and can be used satisfactorily and reliably provided that gasket cement is used in the assembly. The important point is that the apertures in carburettor, manifold and ports line up satisfactorily, so that the gases have an even path along which to flow without any steps or irregularities: from this point of view it is well worth taking great pains to match them up when assembling the engine.

The same goes for the exhaust manifold, which is less critical on the Ford engine than on some others. The ideal is a well-designed free-flow, four-branch manifold, however, and once again these are widely available.

With the engine set up in this manner, with eighty thou. planed off the head, it is possible that you will have some difficulty when it comes to adjusting the rocker clearances, and to overcome this you can fit one-sixteenth in. spacers under the rocker pillars. This will be perfectly adequate for road use, and is in any case a good deal less expensive than the alternative, which is to fit special, shorter push-rods.

This is what we can regard as stage one tuning, and should increase the power output of a 997 c.c. engine to about 60 b.h.p., and that of the 1198 to up to 70 b.h.p.

Stage Two

Tuning beyond this point will require changes to valve and camshaft installations, and before going further into this it would be worth considering exactly what you expect from the car. If low-speed flexibility is important, there is very little point in going on to stage two tuning, since larger inlet valves and/or a change of camshaft to one giving higher lift and an increase in absolute top-end power will inevitably be accompanied by a noticeable reduction in the level of performance available at, say, below 3,000 r.p.m. In the case of some camshaft profiles, the engine will need an extra thousand revs. or so to achieve maximum power, and if you are running with a standard bottom end (in which case you should not exceed 6,500 r.p.m.) this may mean that you have to rev. into the red to get the benefit.

Larger valves can be fitted to all engines, but you must remember that these will only improve top-end performance at some expense to that at the bottom end of the rev-range. If you decide to go ahead and fit them, the valve seats and throats will have to be suitably enlarged: this requires expert use of a seat-cutting tool which isn't, in any case, likely to form part of the equipment of the normal home garage/workshop, and so you will be best off by having this done professionally.

In the 997 and 1200 engines the valves to use are the standard 1500 Cortina G.T. valves with 1.405 inlet and 1.24 exhaust head diameters. The valves themselves can be suitably modified, but this needs a good deal of care since, if you overdo it, the valve will fall to pieces, which is definitely not to be recommended. All Ford valve stems are coated with a black anti-friction, anti-wear finish which, incidentally, covers more of the stem on the inlet valve than on the exhaust and this must be left intact. Metal can be removed also as shown in (Diagram 5).

By the time this point has been reached it will be worth thinking about a change of camshaft and, once again, the Cortina G.T. cam is a good choice for a road car. This will give no appreciable difficulties with idling or smoothness at the bottom end, but will improve the breathing. Alternatively, a rally cam obtainable from most Ford-specialising tuning establishments will also give good performance, and either of these can be used satisfactorily on the road. Use the G.T. distributor.

Engine revs are now the thing to watch, as some camshaft profiles will want to go on to around 7,000 r.p.m. or more before producing maximum power, as we said earlier, and if this sort of crankshaft speed is going to be used as a matter of habit the standard bottom end will not be satisfactory. You will certainly need steel heavy duty main bearing carriers, and it would probably be wise to go in for bottom-end balancing although this probably depends on the amount of money that is spare (remember, though, that bottom-end damage can be umpteen times as expensive) and if you aren't going to use high revs a lot of the time—you probably will—a steel main bearing cap for the centre main would probably be sufficient.

This sort of tuning, properly carried out, will give somewhere around 70 b.h.p. for the 997 engine, and up to an extra 10 b.h.p. for the 1200. For road use, its about as far as you can get on these small engines without severe loss of flexibility, and although there is room for further development, any power increase from now on is going to be expensive, will mean that the engine needs regular stripping if it is going to be reliable, and is best regarded as a competition tune.

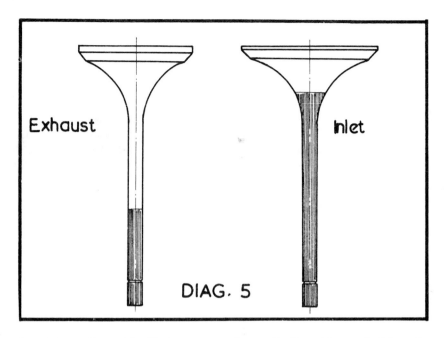

Exhaust

Inlet

DIAG. 5

Stage Three   Competition Tuning

Before we go any further, it is as well to get one thing straight—the amateur is handicapped from the start by all manner of things outside his control. Building an engine which is capable of winning is almost certainly beyond his scope and capabilities, as well as being financially a colossal undertaking. But without access to special parts—some of which are by no means generally available—and a degree of engineering and design knowledge and skill which, if he's got it, puts him outside the world of the amateur, he just is not going to be able to get enough power to win races.

However, let's assume that we're going to build a one-litre racing engine on as small a budget as possible. To begin with, the question of cost means that you've got to start with the three-bearing block instead of the five-bearing block you should use for a racing power unit.

Personally, I would never build another three-bearing engine.

The first thing to do is to get hold of a block. The sensible approach here is to buy a new one, frankly—it only costs £18 or so, and then you are at least certain of the condition of the bores. If you are using an old block and the bores are worn you'll have to give the matter a lot of thought. Simply boring them out won't really solve the problem, because you can't get racing pistons in the normal oversizes. Once you've got the block right, however, the next step, on a three-bearing engine, is to fit steel main bearing caps, obtainable from Ford racing specialists, and have them line-bored 15 thou. oversize to accept racing main-bearing shells. At the same time it is advisable, unless you are using a brand-new block, to fit new bearing-cap bolts.

Assuming that you are building this engine from the bottom up, so to speak, the next thing you want is a crankshaft.

There's no problem here—you must use a new one. Second-hand crankshafts, or used crankshafts, represent virtual suicide on a racing engine, and the same goes for the con-rods. Obviously you want the best you can get, and the best plan is to select the most suitable one from the stock of your local Ford dealer if he's friendly. If he's not, you'll have to try another Ford dealer! What you are looking for is a lack of porosity, good radii on all the journals and a "clean" appearance generally. The same goes for the rods—the point to watch here, as well as all the other points, is concentricity of the big and small ends.

It is worthwhile matching the rods for weight. Apart from choosing four rods which are as close to each other in weight as possible, you can "adjust" them by grinding metal off the squared section on each end of the rod—it is provided for the purpose, and you won't have to worry about weakening the rods by doing so. (See Diagram 7).

Do not polish the rods, because if you do you will weaken them, and make them liable to cracking.

Flywheel and Clutch

Use the normal 105E flywheel. You can have it lightened, but frankly, within the safe limits of lightening it probably won't show much advantage. It would be better to have the crank and flywheel balanced as a complete assembly, but, here again, normal Ford tolerances aren't all that bad, and if it is a matter of finance you could probably get away with it, leaving it untouched.

The cheapest clutch you can fit which will hold the power is the GT Cortina pressure-plate and driven plate—the best of all is the diaphragm clutch, with competition driven plate—you can get these from Ford tuning specialists—if you can afford it. The normal Ford clutch plate, however, can tend to disintegrate after a bit of hard use.

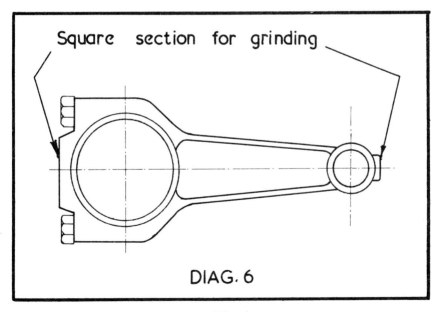

Square section for grinding

DIAG. 6

Pistons

There isn't much point in using the standard Ford ones—they are a bit on the heavy side to begin with, and apart from that would probably crack under competition strains. Hepolite make die-cast alloy pistons with flat tops which are not too expensive—you can, on pukka racing pistons of slipper-type, spend fifty or sixty quid a set. The Hepolite ones are easily obtainable from Ford tuning specialists, but to all practical intents and purposes they will only fit standard bore sizes.

When you get to this stage you can fit it all up and then measure how far the pistons are below the top deck of the block when they are at top dead centre. According to what this is, you have the block face ground off so that you get the pistons flush with the face. In most cases it won't be more than 45 thou. to come off.

Camshafts

With standard crank and rods the maximum rev-limit is 8,000 r.p.m., and both crank and rods should be crack-tested every 200 miles. This rev-limit immediately dictates the sort of camshaft you can use, and you don't necessarily want the hottest you can buy. What you do want, however, is something that will be pulling by the time you have got to 6,000 r.p.m., and which will then carry on up to 8,000 r.p.m. before the power drops off.

When you fit the new camshaft you will also have to fit new cam-followers, but the camshaft drive itself usually gives very little trouble up to 8,000 r.p.m. At about eight-four, however, the links may fall out and the whole thing disintegrates, so you want to keep your eye on the rev-counter!

Provided you pay attention to one or two points you shouldn't run into any lubrication problems. The first precaution is to replace the four-pint sump fitted as standard with the 6¼-pint sump from the 1500. This is quite satisfactory as it comes, but if you want to you can fit a baffle-plate to prevent surge—don't forget to leave an aperture for the pick-up and relief valve return pipes. The baffle is something you can quite easily make up yourself, out of 16 or 18 gauge plate.

This brings us to the oil pump. Once again, the standard component is quite satisfactory for use under racing conditions, and all you've got to do is to fit a modified relief-valve spring—you'll have to buy this, but most reputable tuning firms keep them in stock. Another good mod is to block off the oil filter-by-pass valve, to make sure that all the oil goes through the filter. Bearing in mind that you should change it after every race, the standard filter is O.K. When you fit the filter, however, make sure that the filter bowl is free from any sharp edges on the top flange, and if you can find one, fit a thick-walled bowl (you'll probably have to "borrow" one from an older engine because at some point the size was changed). There is a good deal of latitude on the Bowl location, so make sure you get it centralised on the rubber ring or it may cut the rubber. I have, in fact, stressed this point because I have had an engine failure through this very point—the rubber ring was cut and subsequently let go all the oil.

The standard water pump will do the job all right, but you must replace the crankshaft pulley with a one-piece type of cast iron, obtainable from tuning shops. The standard pulley is a metal pressing in two halves, and at high r.p.m. these tend to fly apart—I have seen cars with the halves of the pulley firmly embedded in the radiator and the battery.

26

Courtesy Ford Motor Company

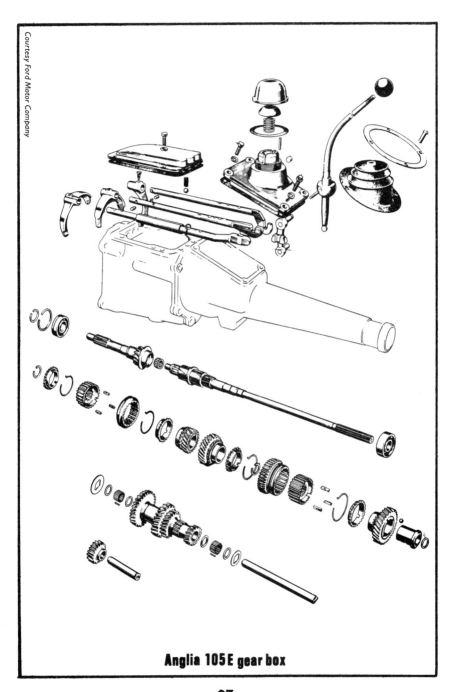

Anglia 105E gear box

filter. Bearing in mind that you should change it after every race, the standard filter is O.K. When you fit the filter, however, make sure that the filter bowl is free from any sharp edges on the top flange, and if you can find one, fit a thick-walled bowl (you'll probably have to "borrow" one from an older engine because at some point the size was changed). There is a good deal of latitude on the Bowl location, so make sure you get it centralised on the rubber ring or it may cut the rubber.

The standard water pump will do the job all right, but you must replace the crankshaft pulley with a one-piece type of cast iron, obtainable from tuning shops. The standard pulley is a metal pressing in two halves, and at high r.p.m. these tend to fly apart—you can see cars with the halves of the pulley firmly embedded in the radiator and the battery.

You can also use the standard distributor —the advance curve needn't bother you, because with an engine that doesn't start working properly until it reaches 6,000 r.p.m. you are well outside the curve anyway. To prevent "point-bounce" you should fit a set of Lucas competition points. Lucas do, of course, make a special racing distributor, which already has the heavy duty points plus one or two other items, which costs about £8.

It is absolutely essential to fit an oil-cooler. A suitable one isn't hard to find —several types are available in kits which involve an adaptor fitted between the oil-filler bowl and the oil-pump body. This is coupled up with suitable hose to a light alloy radiator mounted in front of the car—the best place is directly in front of the water rad.

Cylinder Head

You've got a problem straight away here, because the first thing to do is to find a head that you can grind down enough, without going through to the water jacket. Obviously, you need to make sure that you've got a high compression head to start with—this is the 8·9 to 1 head fitted as standard to domestic 997 c.c. engines, or on the 1200 it is 8·7 to 1. On some export models a low-compression head is fitted of 7·5 or 7·3 to 1 respectively, but this is just a point to be watched rather than worried about. When you are selecting one you run into the problem, and there is unfortunately no rule of thumb which can be applied, and there isn't really a convenient measurement which can be used. Roughly speaking, you want a head with the smallest possible water hole adjacent to the plug hole while the land from the plug edge of the combustion chamber to the water hole wants to be as big as possible. (See Diagram 8).

There's no real way round this except experience. Trial and error will probably have to be the answer—take 100 thou. off the head, put a gasket over it and then see how much land is left between the gasket and the water hole. The minimum required to hold the gasket is about ⅜ in., and all you can hope to do is take off as much as you can. It is fair to say that you can never take off enough—the ideal is something around 200 thou., but you are most unlikely to be able to do this unless you are very lucky with your heads.

The next move is to modify the chamber. Take the head, put a gasket over it and scribe a line round the bore hole, which gives you the outer limits. Then grind the chamber to a heart shape, as in Diagram 9.

This head work is one of the biggest limiting factors for the amateur. All you can really hope for is a compression ratio of up to 10·5 to 1, and you can see what you'll be up against when you realise that professional tuners used to go up to 13 to 1.

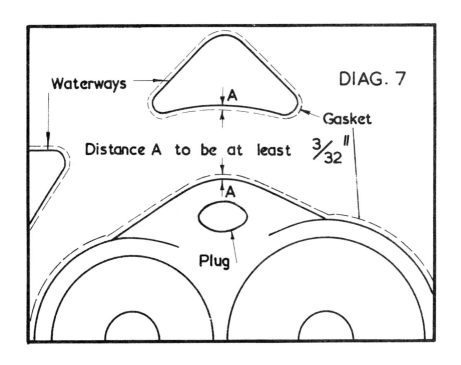

Waterways

DIAG. 7

Gasket

Distance A to be at least $\frac{3}{32}''$

Plug

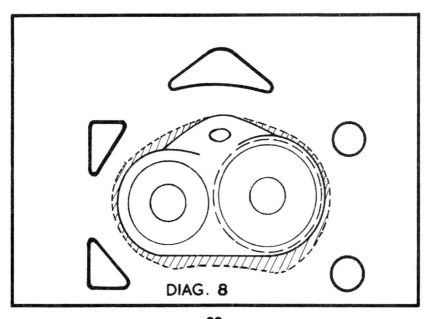

DIAG. 8

The inlet ports should be opened out to 1·050 in., and the exhaust ports left standard. The valve pockets must be opened up to take inlet valves of 1·4 in. and exhaust valves of 1·25 in.—for cheapness you can use GT valves, which are satisfactory up to 8,000 r.p.m. provided they are fitted with special springs. If, on the other hand, you are going to fit special valves you will have to fit bronze valve guides into the head if you are going to get a reasonable guide life. Most of the special valves available involve machining the head to take special valve springs, retainers and collets. The valve throats must be nicely blended into the ports so that you get a smooth flow rather than a sudden change of direction, and the valves can be lightened, in the same way as has already been suggested doing them for road use, but very, very judiciously, because of the hammering they get at high r.p.m. Less metal, if anything, should come off the valves on a racing engine, unless they are of special material.

If you are going to use GT valves with single springs, the standard valve gear will give no trouble. But if you are using double springs and special valves you must use a strengthened rocker shaft assembly, which you can get from tuning specialists. A set of shorter push-rods (tuning specialists again) will be essential, and you won't be able to adjust the tappets. Valve clearance will depend on the cam, and the firm from which you buy it will be able to advise you on this point.

So far as sparking plugs are concerned, the grade you want is Champion L5 7R, or the equivalent from another manufacturer.

There's no argument about carburation —you want two Weber 40 DCOE instruments, on a suitable manifold. This is the ideal set-up and anything else will give poorer performance. When setting up the carbs you want 32 mm.

chokes with 200 needle valves, 130 main jets, 160 air correction jets, 45 F9 slow running jets, 35 pump jets and F16 emulsion tubes.

Exhaust Manifold

This should be made up with the primary pipes—one from each port—of a minimum bore of 1¼ in. These feed into the secondary pipes, which must have a minimum bore of 1⅜ in., and the tailpipe minimum bore should be 1⅞ in. Lengths are critical, and the best seem to be 15 in. for primaries and secondaries, and 34 in. for the tail pipe, but you may have to work out a compromise here because it won't be easy to accommodate that much plumbing in the space available.

If money is tight you can use a GT manifold, which is as cheap as you can get at a tenner, and while the pipes are reasonably satisfactory the lengths aren't as good as all that.

When you are fitting the manifold, remember that the standard exhaust manifold gasket is unsatisfactory—it will blow after quite a short life, and you'll need a special one which most tuning firms sell.

To this specification you could build a 1000 c.c. or 1,200 c.c. engine giving 85 or 95 b.h.p. respectively: both would be capable of being revved to 8,000 r.p.m. and the peak power would be at about 7,000 r.p.m. The 1200 can be made to produce a bit more power with 1·5 in. inlet and 1·3 in. exhaust valves, and larger chokes and so on on the carbs— 34 mm. chokes, 140 main jets, 160 air correction jets and the others about the same. Then you would get about 100-102 b.h.p., and in fact if you tried hard enough, using, say, second-hand carbs and so on and watching costs pretty closely, you could build an engine like this for as little as £100.

Transmission

The standard Anglia/Anglia Super transmission consists of a $7\frac{1}{4}$ in. clutch mating
the engine to a four-speed gearbox. The
box fitted to the 997 c.c. car has synchromesh on the upper three forward ratios
only, but the 1198 c.c. model has synchro
on all four, while ratios differ slightly
between the two, bottom gear being a
slightly higher (numerically lower) ratio
on the 1198 than on the 997. The final
drive ratio on the larger car was always
the 4.125, giving 15.7 m.p.h./1,000 r.p.m.
in top gear with standard wheels and
tyres. The 997 Anglia, however, was
made with both the 4.125 and also a
4.44 final drive, and in the latter case all
gears a lower (numerically higher) and
on cars so equipped (from 1966) the
overall gearing gives only 14.7 m.p.h./
1,000 r.p.m. in top gear.

The gearboxes are interchangeable, although when fitting the 997 c.c. car with
an all-synchromesh gearbox it is also
necessary to use the shorter propshaft
from the Anglia 1200. However, a better
bet for a modified car is the gearbox
from the late Cortina GT/Cortina Lotus/
Corsair V4, which can also be fitted as a
straight swap (provided the prop-shaft
point is observed) and which have uprated second gears to give less of a gap
between second and third.

With a significant power increase, it is
likely that the 4.4 final drive will be too
low when considered in terms of cruising
and maximum speeds, so that unless
fairly dramatic acceleration is being
sought after the 4.125 is probably the
best bet. As well as these two, a wide
range of final drives is available from
tuning specialists or from the Ford
Performance Centre.

The standard clutch, assuming that it
is in good condition, will usually be
satisfactory for mild tuning, but where
you are getting real power from either
the 997 or the 1200 cars, the best answer
is the Cortina GT clutch, as mentioned
earlier.

Suspension, etc. and brakes

The standard Anglia suspension will not
give adequate standards of roadholding
and handling with a modified car, and
the brakes, if you don't do something to
improve them, will certainly not be able
to cope with the higher speeds. For mild
tuning, the suspension can in fact be left
alone provided that the dampers are in
first-class condition, but any improvement in performance will definitely require an improved standard of braking.
Although it comes fairly late in the book,
it must be stressed that any real tuning
work must be looked on as a second
part in a programme which begins with
attention to these two departments:
getting the handling and stopping right
is the real number one priority, and this
point cannot be made too often.

The usual first step in suspension modifying is to lower the car all round. To
deal with the front, a cheap way out is
to cut approximately $1\frac{1}{2}$ coils of the
front springs. This is not quite as easy
as it sounds, because the end has to be
reformed in a particular way or you
will be unable to relocate the spring
properly when you come to put it all
back together. You will be best off with
a visit to the local blacksmith or any
small engineering firm with a forge, and
get the end reformed exactly as it was
in standard form.

This will lower the front end by about
$1\frac{1}{4}$ in., and will also give a slight
increase in spring rate—in other words,
the spring will then be a bit stiffer:
harder, if you like. When you re-fit the
shortened springs you'll find that it is
necessary to reset the track to the
standard setting.

As an alternative you can buy a special
front spring from some of the tuning
firms made up to a shorter length and to
a thicker wire gauge. These cost around
£6 a pair, and give an increase in spring
rate of up to thirty per cent. This much
reduces the roll stiffness at the front,
but has a negligible effect on riding

31

comfort—an important point for road cars although it doesn't necessarily apply to racing machines, where we are less concerned with comfort than with the best possible road-holding and cornering power.

Before we go on to the rear end, it will be worth giving a brief run-down on how the front suspension is made up. As you will see as soon as you look at the car, the basis is two vertical coil spring/damper units, each of which is mounted in a rubber bearing at the top, fixed to a reinforced bracket on the body. At the bottom end of each unit a track control arm is pivoted, of which the outer ends are connected by the anti-roll bar. The inner ends have rubber bushes to the front cross-member of the "chassis", and ball-joints on the outer ends allow the steering joints to swivel, and move up and down as the suspension does its job. To connect the steering arms to a transverse rod there are adjustable track-rods, and the transverse rod itself moves on swinging links which are in fact the drop arm and an idler arm, which are kept parallel. Wheel bearings and toe-in or toe-out of the front wheels are adjustable, but the camber, caster and inclination angles of the kingpins are fixed during manufacture and cannot be adjusted.

You can (if you have a friendly Ford dealer) get special clips with which to hold the coil springs in compression while you are dismantling and reassembling the suspension units, and this is a job which needs a good deal of care. Quite apart from the fact that you'll find that the springs take a good deal of compressing, if one of them should "get away" while you are working on it it will do a lot of damage as it goes—probably to you, and certainly to the workshop! Whenever you dismantle the front suspension you should check the wheel alignment once you have put it back together again.

Rear Suspension

Once again the usual first step is to lower the suspension, and the cheapest and as it happens the best way of doing this is to fit a spacer between the axle and the spring itself. Jack up the car, and lower it on to stands, then take off the wheels at the rear jacking points. The "U"-bolts which attach the axle to the springs have self-locking nuts, and if you examine them carefully you will see that they are not identical. Suitable spacers and longer replacement "U"-bolts are obtainable from most Ford tuning specialists.

The disadvantage of this—one which applies to any method of lowering the suspension—is that the rear suspension will now bottom if you put any sort of load in the back, whether it is people in the back seats or luggage in the boot. To overcome this you can replace the bump-stop rubbers with Aeon hollow rubber springs, which do a great job in this respect. Once again, they are easily obtainable.

Another method of lowering the rear suspension is to have the rear springs de-cambered, or flattened, by a forge, or the local blacksmith. This is an going to be rather expensive and, in expensive and time-wasting method of lowering compared with fitting spacers, which is not only quick, but which allows you to put the car back to standard any time you like.

However you do it, it isn't advisable to lower the car by more than 1½ in. because of the bump-stops: if you lower it by more than this it is quite easy to put the axle-housing through the floor, which isn't a lot of good. The other point to remember is that the 1½ in. lowering represents a comparison with the standard ride-height of the car—if yours has done a bit of mileage and the springs have all settled, you should check the ride-height of a new one and lower your car against that.

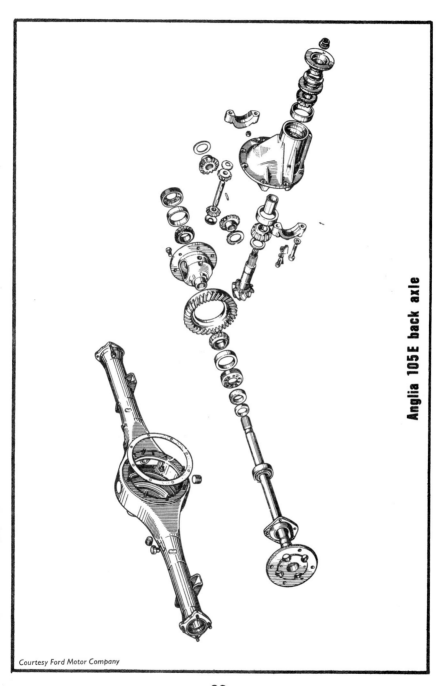

Anglia 105E back axle

Courtesy Ford Motor Company

33

Dampers are the next point. The best thing is to start again, replacing the rear shock- absorbers with adjustable units and the front ones with dampers using harder- setting valves. The best ones for the job are the Armstrong Firmaride, with the Adjustaride at the back; Konis, of course, also make suitable dampers.

It is quite easy to stiffen the front end with an anti-roll bar—all you need to do on an Anglia is to fit another bar, identical to the standard one, and simply clamp them together. This reduces body-roll but will, of course, increase the amount of understeer. You can reduce this again by giving the front wheels negative camber, but since there is no adjustment for this you will have to have a suitable front suspension cross-member—one which has been re-drilled on a jig and strengthened appropriately. This is fitted in place of the existing cross-member, and since you are unlikely to have access to a suitable jig this is something you will have to buy.

Alternatively, the complete Cortina GT front cross-member can be fitted. This will give a small amount of negat camber, but has the further advantage that you will also "win" front disc brakes, which are really the only answer when it comes to satisfactory braking for a quick Anglia. You can improve the existing drum brakes on the car by fitting hard linings, such as Ferodo VG95s, which will be more efficient and resistant to fade when the car is stopping from high speeds. At low speeds, when the linings are cold, you'll find that linings of this type need firmer pedal pressures, and to overcome this you can fit a servo. This device is fairly widely misunderstood: it does not on its own give improved braking: it merely gives, in effect, more braking for a given pedal pressure—it takes some of the work out of moving the system. Fitting harder linings can do no more than make the existing brakes as good as they can be within the limits of their own physical properties and dimensions: bearing in mind that they were designed only to be effective on a car with the Anglia's standard performance, it really boils down to a complete change if you are going to get really good results. The only complete answer, really, is disc front brakes, which you can achieve either by grafting on the complete front end of a disc-braked car, such as the Cortina, or by using one of the disc brake conversions such as that marketed by Allard Motor Co. Again, you will probably find, if your Anglia is very quick, that you need an anti-fade type of pad even discs, and a good example is the Ferodo DS11.

Wheels and tyres have a considerable effect on roadholding, and this is a worthwhile improvement even if the rest of the suspension is left unmodified. Lotus-Cortina $5\frac{1}{2}$ in. section rims can be fitted straight on at the rear while at the front a quarter-inch spacer will be necessary. Alternatively, you could use any professionally-widened wheel of similar dimensions and with similar offsets, while so far as tyres are concerned, for road Anglias the answer is 165 section radials.

CHAPTER 4
tuning the 1500 cortina classic & capri

This section deals with Cortinas up to the 1500 c.c. version and does not include the cross-flow head series of engines. The Capri referred to is the long-tailed "personal car" of 1962-64, and should not be confused with the cross-flow engined car of the same name introduced in 1969. Cortinas fitted with the 1198 c.c. engine can be dealt with exactly as outlined for the 1198 c.c. Anglia Super since the power unit etc. is identical, as is the gearbox: apart from the body shell itself, the only significant difference from the point of view of this book lies in the fact that the car was fitted with disc brakes at the front, as were the Capri and Classic models.

The most popular Cortina for the tuning brigade was the 116E version, with 1498 c.c. o.h.v. engine featuring five main bearings for the crankshaft, resulting in a much more rigid bottom end capable of being more highly tuned with less danger of serious unreliability than the smaller three-bearing engines; this was the engine from which the twin overhead camshaft Lotus-Cortina engine was developed.

A basic stage one tune for this engine would be to bring it roughly to Cortina GT power output: it must be stressed that although this is not difficult, the necessary modifications do not in fact bring the engine to complete GT specifications, since this involves stronger pistons, lead-indium bearings and, of course, a stronger clutch to cope with the extra power.

As usual, the head is the first place to start. Better results will be achieved by reworking the existing head than by simply fitting the GT head, although this will provide a small increase in power. But the head can be treated as for the Anglia component; if left as standard, its basically superior breathing characteristics will allow a slight increase —a maximum of about 4 b.h.p.—with the addition of improved carburation, but for a significant increase in power the combustion chambers must be modified and the compression ratio raised by machining the head face.

With the compression ratio at 9.5 to 1 or thereabouts, ports and chambers polished and equalised for volume, Cortina GT valves can be fitted and should be equipped with heavy-duty valve springs to raise the valve-bounce point to 7,000 r.p.m. With a 28/36 DCD Weber carburettor (fitted as standard to the GT engine) on a suitable cast-alloy

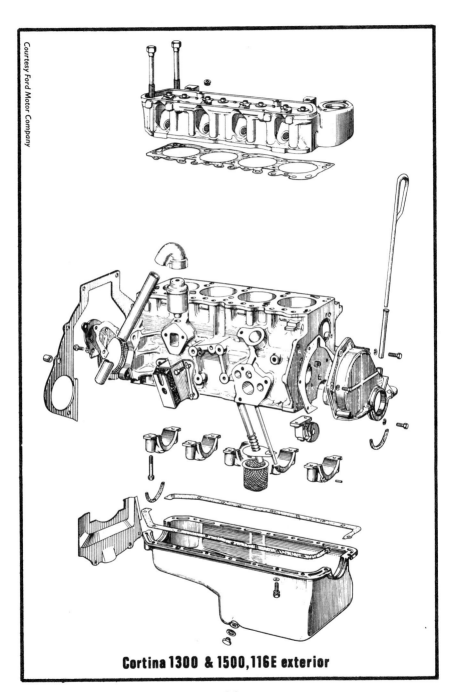

Courtesy Ford Motor Company

Cortina 1300 & 1500, 116E exterior

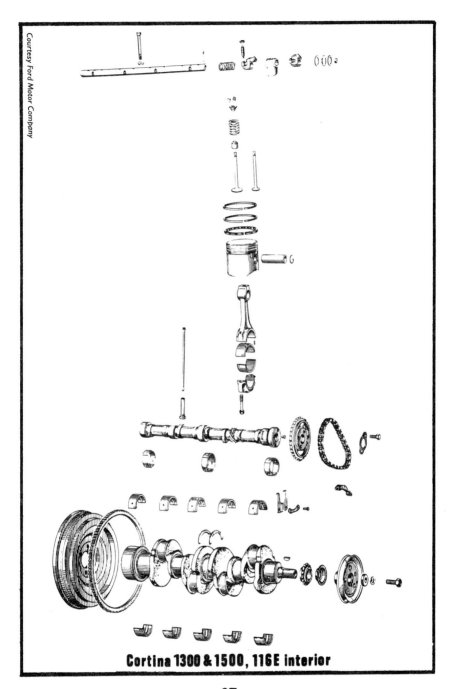

Courtesy Ford Motor Company

Cortina 1300 & 1500, 116E interior

inlet manifold, a four-branch exhaust manifold and GT silencer, power output should be approximately 74 b.h.p.

Stage Two

The first step for more advanced tuning would be to fit the GT camshaft and distributor which, if added to the Stage One set-up outlined above, would raise power output to around 80 b.h.p.
However, this is only a first step in the more advanced tuning of these engines, which will produce real power. Before going in too deep, therefore, the engine itself will need to be strengthened if it started as a normal 1500: preferably, Stage Two should be carried out only on GT engines although provided heavy-duty bearings, such as Vandervell, are used, together with stronger and, preferably, lighter pistons, the normal 1500 can be treated in the same way.
Using the same head specification as above, the GT camshaft can be replaced with a competition cam, such as the A2, A3 or the Ford WEC, which is the one used in their push-rod engined rally cars. This will possibly require a change of distributor. The bottom end needs careful preparation for this stage of tune, and it goes without saying that all bearings and bearing cap bolts must be replaced with brand-new components. At the same time, it is probably worth fitting heavy-duty main bearing caps, which must be line-bored.
The 28/36 DCD Weber and manifold should be replaced by twin 40 DCOE Webers and manifolds, which will themselves provide, when properly set up, another 8-10 b.h.p. when used together with the rest of the engine specification suggested above. Total power output, in fact, will be something over 90 b.h.p. and the car's top speed should be comfortably over the ton. A snag is that it will rev far beyond the safe continuous limit of 6,500 r.p.m., but with the 7,000 r.p.m. valve springs serious over-revving will

be prevented, while peak power should develop at about six thousand and you will be able to run a little beyond this in the gears. A more satisfactory method of limiting r.p.m., of course, is to fit a limiting cut-out in the distributor, which is the method employed on production Lotuses.

Stage Three   Competition Tuning

Much of what we have already said in respect of the 997 c.c. and 1198 c.c. engines can be applied to this power unit. The compression ratio can be further increased by removing an additional 20 thou. from the head face to make a total of 100 thou.—bear in mind that, as we mentioned earlier, not every head will stand this much metal being removed. The combustion chambers must again be balanced and polished and the valve seats must be recut to accept larger valves of 1.56 ins. diameter (inlet) and 1.35 ins. diameter (exhaust), with 30 degree inlet valve seats and 45 degree exhaust. Special silicone single valve springs must be fitted and the valve guides should be replaced by special bronze ones for increased life.
The valve gear will be subjected to pretty severe strains and it is advisable to fit a two-piece rocker shaft, obtainable from Ford Performance Centre or from specialist tuning firms.
Connecting rods should be Lotus-Cortina 125E pattern and should be carefully selected and matched for weight, but you can adjust any slight variations by removing metal from the flat portion at each end of the rod (which is what is there for, anyway). Once again, rods should not be polished. It goes without saying that, as for the 997/1198 engines, the crankshaft used on a racing power unit must be brand-new, never a reground component, and the best type is the improved 116B component which superseded the 116E. The normal 1500 flywheel, which is a

Courtesy Ford Motor Company

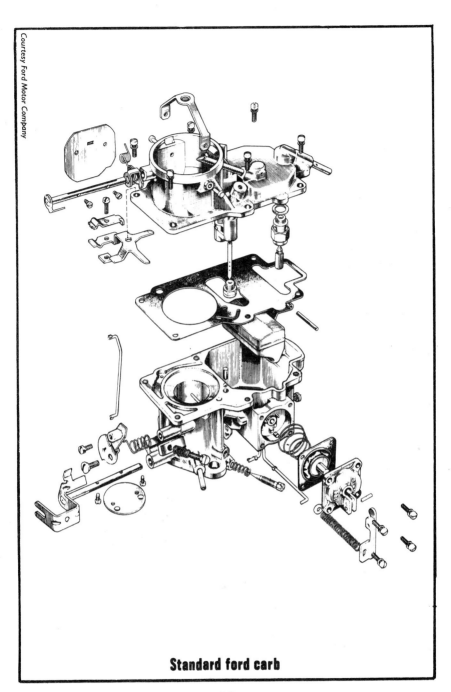

Standard ford carb

very heavy component, should be replaced by one from the 105E engine and the complete bottom-end assembly, including the clutch, must be balanced: a set of five steel main bearing caps must be used, with new bolts, and these must be line-bored 15 thou. oversize to accept racing bearing shells. A special racing clutch is desirable, but certainly you can't expect to hold the power with anything less than the Cortina GT clutch: preferably use the diaphragm-type unit with a competition driven plate.

Pistons should be replaced, and the Hepolite die-cast alloy pistons with flat tops are satisfactory and not too costly: generally speaking ,however, these will fit only standard bores.

Shortened pushrods will be necessary—you can't really expect to get away with the packing shims on a proper racing motor. The WEC cam can be used or, alternatively, a full-race cam is available which will give power between 5,500-8,000 r.p.m. The best carburettors to use are 45 DCOE Webers, and, as we said in the Anglia section, it isn't really practical to attempt to give detailed settings. As a start, however, you should try the following:

Chokes	36 mm
Needle valves	200
Main jets	160
Air correction jets	180
Pump jets	35
Slow-run jets	45 F9 or F6
Emulsion tubes	F16

Properly set up, this engine should be producing up to 130 b.h.p.

The five-bearing 1300 c.c. engine, introduced in 1967 with the Mk. II Cortina bodyshell, develops around 55 b.h.p. in standard trim. The head and valves are the same as those on the 1500, and the GT camshaft can be fitted. Capacity can be increased by reboring to 85 mm (which, of course, means new pistons) but this is something which needs a bit of thought as not all blocks will stand it. If it can be done, however, it'll give a capacity of around 1400 c.c. and with reworked head, GT cam and Weber 28/36 DCD you'll get about 75 b.h.p. and a substantial improvement in torque.

Transmission

All the cars we are considering in this section have four-speed gearboxes with synchromesh on all forward gears. However, the Classic, Capri and Mk. I Cortinas suffer, so far as improved performance is concerned, from very low second gear ratios which leave a wide gap between second and third. Some early Cortinas may have been fitted with an uprated second gear cluster which was at that time available but which has since been discontinued, but from 1967 all Cortinas share the same, closer, ratios. This is the gearbox fitted to the V4 Corsair GT and 2000E and, subsequently, to Lotus-Cortina, etc. These gears can be fitted to earlier Cortinas and are the best answer, since they are nicely spaced and very robust.

Apart from this, Ford Performance Centre can supply two other close-ratio gear sets, one intended for rally and fast road use, while the other is suitable for circuit racing only and is available as either a set of internals or as a complete gearbox.

Final drive ratios can be changed by swapping the crown-wheel and pinion set for any of the wide range available: those normally fitted to production cars were either 3.9, 4.1, 3.7 or 3.5, the last two being used on the V4 Corsairs, but, again, Ford Performance Centre can supply 4.44, 4.7, 5.14 and 5.57 to 1 ratios for particular purposes. Obviously, a lower (numerically higher) ratio will give improved top gear and possibly overall acceleration, while a higher (numerically lower) ratio will give a higher road speed per 1,000 r.p.m. engine speed. Bear in mind, though, that

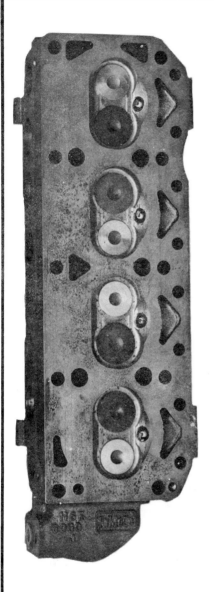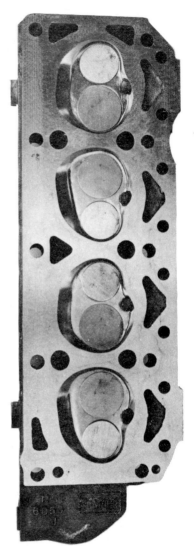

(left) Standard 116E (1500) head,
(right) the same head gas–flowed and skimmed

Courtesy Ford Motor Company

Cut-away Cortina

changing the final drive will raise or lower all the ratios in the box, and generally speaking, ratios lower (numerically higher) than 4.4 to 1 are not usually practical for road use. For instance, Ford's 4.4 ratio gives a top speed of around 95 m.p.h. at 6,000 r.p.m.; to reach the same maximum with the 5.5, you'd need to be pulling 7,500 r.p.m.; which simply is NOT ON with the standard bottom end.

For competition purposes, a limited-slip differential is desirable and for serious competition, it is essential. Without going into the hows and whys, the object of this component is to transmit full power to one wheel even if the opposite wheel is spinning under power.

Suspension, etc. and brakes

Much of what we have already said for the Anglia applies just as much, if not more so, to the Cortina models we are discussing here. Lowering the suspension is, once again, the usual starting point, and you can use the same method on the Cortina as we suggested on the Anglia, front and rear. On any well-used Cortina, you should check the ride height before you start lowering, since after considerable mileages springs will settle and the car may well be lower than it was originally to start with. A maximum of 1½ ins. is again all that is permissible for road-use cars unless you want to lose the privilege of being able to carry back-seat passengers or luggage in the boot.

So far as dampers are concerned, again the same goes as for the Anglia—Armstrong adjustables on the back, Firmarides on the front are the best answer.

On earlier models not fitted with the rear radius arms, you can get some advantage by fitting the stouter Lotus-Cortina anti-roll bar. On later models, which do have the radius arms at the back, it is better to remove these and keep to the standard roll-bar—removing

the radius arms has the effect of softening the rear suspension, which then has characteristics more in phase with those of the front end at no sacrifice to riding comfort. The radius arm itself has very little effect on axle tramp, which can be reduced on the Cortina by removing the bush from the front end of the rear spring and replacing it with a bush of a harder composition (which you can get from Ford specialists) or by using an Anglia bush plus a suitable sleeve to compensate for the different diameter.

On all Cortinas except the Lotus-Cortina, you can get negative camber on the front wheels by fitting Lotus-Cortina track control arms.

For road use, the best wheels are 5½ in. rims: Lotus-Cortina or 1600E wheels will do very well, while the tyres to give best results are 175 section radials. Fitting these wheels and tyres alone, incidentally, is a worthwhile thing to do and gives a significant improvement in roadholding.

If you are seriously considering racing we can assume to start with that the Cortina in question is either a GT or a Lotus-type, as nothing else is worth thinking about. The front suspension can be lowered by up to two inches, using special front springs, and at the same time the front camber must be changed to racing settings by means of the special cross-member we have mentioned several times already in this chapter. A standard Lotus-Cortina roll-bar must be fitted, and you will make some improvement by removing the rubber mountings in which the roll-bar normally works and replacing them with spherical joints or self-lubricating bearings, which you will have to have made up out of some suitably hard material such as phosphor-bronze. The object of the exercise is to ensure absolutely positive location of the roll-bar.

At the rear end, standard rear springs are satisfactory. The spring eye bush should be changed to one of a much harder material, and the rear dampers should obviously be changed for adjustable pattern units. Radius arms must be fitted to the axle—those already fitted to later models are quite useless for racing, and the mounting points must in any case be raised to the top of the axle-tube. Longer radius arms than the standard ones are necessary, too, and they must be mounted higher-up on the chassis, which will involve cutting slots in the floor pan.

Seven-inch rim wheels must be fitted, with a minimum size racing tyre of 5·50.

So far as the Cortina brakes are concerned, the drum-braked model can be treated in exactly the same way as the Anglia—you can fit harder linings alone, or a disc-brake conversion plus harder linings at the back, or harder linings and a servo. You can also fit GT disc brakes to the front, but this is rather more than simply swapping over the drums for the discs. Hubs and suspension units are also different on the GT, and you will therefore have to change these as well as fitting the discs and calipers. On GT models, the brakes can be improved by fitting Ferodo DS 11 front pads and VG95 rear linings, or the equivalent grade from another manufacturer, together with a brake servo unit. The Girling Powerstop booster is deservedly popular and is easy to fit—the complete kit is provided with full instructions and it isn't by any means a big job.

The Lotus-Cortina, of course, has all these things—discs, servo and so on—and the only improvement you need make on this model is in the fitting of competition pads and linings.

If you are building up a car from second-hand parts it ought to be stressed here that if you are increasing the power of the brakes you must also give a bit of thought to those parts of the car which are going to have to work harder because of it—the suspension units, axle attachments and so on. You must make sure that all these parts are in first class-condition—this is vital,

44

CHAPTER 5
the 1600 crossflow cortina

The crossflow engine design, also known as "bowl-in-piston", or the Heron head, has several advantages and is not by any means peculiar to Ford. Its significant features are found in the porting arrangements and in combustion chamber location: the inlet ports, with manifolding and carburettor, are on the opposite side of the head to the exhaust ports and manifolding (and, incidentally, the opposite side to those on earlier engines) so that a flow of mixture goes into the combustion chamber through a downward sloping inlet tract, flows across the chamber and out the other side. Hence crossflow. At the same time, the downward path of the inlet tract obviously argues a low-sited combustion chamber, and on these engines this is formed in the piston crown, which is deeply dished, while the head itself has a completely flat face. Hence bowl-in-piston. Actually, this is an over-generalisation: GT heads have a slight cavity in them above the chamber itself, but the actual combustion chamber is still machined into the piston crown. A similar approach can be found on, for example, Rover 2000 and Audi engines, and is a popular diesel-engine layout. Advantages include improved breathing and combustion: the valve openings are not masked to anything like so great an extent as on otherwise similar engines by the combustion chamber walls, while turbulence is improved through the ability of the incoming mixture to emerge from the inlet valve's unmasked opening in all directions at once, further swirl being imparted by the broad top land of the piston as it nears t.d.c. Flame travel is more or less equal in all directions and the engine can also run on a leaner fuel/air mixture so that it should be more economical than an otherwise similar engine of comparable size and power output.

All this is very well, but it does make life a little more difficult for the engine tuner, however. The main disadvantage is that the compression ratio is governed by the volume of the piston cavity: it can be marginally increased by planing the head, but since the latter is flat the removal of significant amounts of metal is impossible since it would bring the valves dangerously close to the pistons. The absolute maximum which can be removed is about 30 thou., while a minimum clearance between valves and pistons at maximum lift of 0.005 ins. must be maintained.

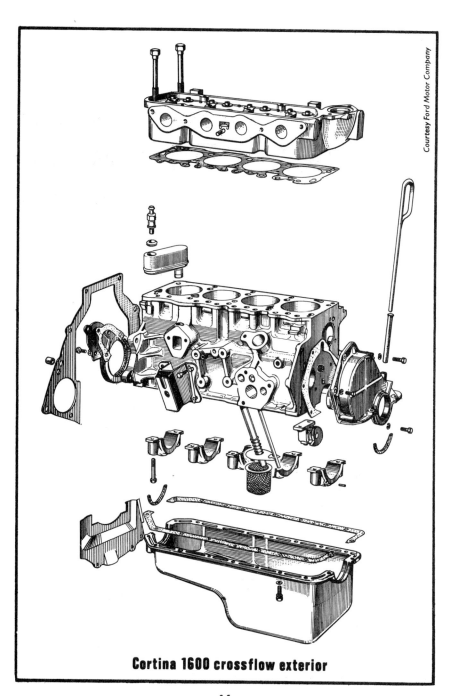

Courtesy Ford Motor Company

Cortina 1600 crossflow exterior

Courtesy Ford Motor Company

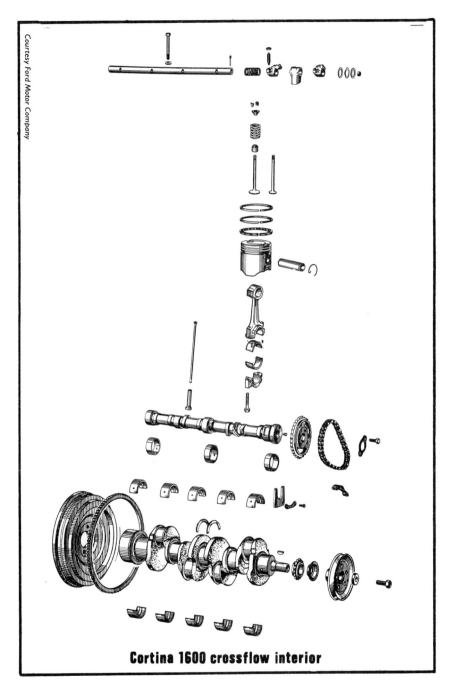

Cortina 1600 crossflow interior

Inlet ports can be polished, but should not be enlarged since the metal is already fairly thin in this area. Normal 1600 engines can with advantage be fitted with the GT head, valves, manifold and carburettor: if you fit the GT camshaft and a good exhaust system as well it is possible to get around 90-95 b.h.p., which represents a substantial increase for the normal 1600: similar mods on the GT, which obviously already has the right valves, manifold, carb and so on, will still show a worthwhile improvement in performance.

So far as the GT engine is concerned, port polishing, plus twin 40 DCOE Weber carbs on a proprietary manifold and a rally cam, such as the Ford WEC, will give up to 110 b.h.p., which argues a performance roughly similar to that of the 1968 twin-cam Cortina.

This, however, is about as far as you can go. Further modifications would involve special pistons, and while there is theoretically no objection to increasing the capacity as far as the block is concerned, bear in mind also that the wide-bore pistons you use will also have to have the combustion chambers machined into them—these just aren't available unless you have them specially made, at a cost which makes the whole project ludicrous—you'd probably find it cheaper to buy a Lamborghini anyway!

Transmission

Transmission on the 1600 crossflow Cortinas can be treated exactly as for the previous models, except that a diaphragm-spring clutch is fitted, for which competition centre-plates are necessary if serious tuning is being considered. The alternative final drive ratios are equally applicable to this model, and the gearbox is, again, the close-ratio 2000E box.

Suspension and brakes, etc.

There are no significant differences here between 1600 crossflow cars and the 1500 series. However, it is worth noting that 1600 GT and 1600 E models are fitted as standard with $5\frac{1}{2}$ in. width rims, the 1600E having the attractive Ro-Style wheels as standard wear. Tyres, again, for road use are best at 175 section radials. The brakes can be fitted with harder Ferodo DS11 front pads and VG95/1 rear linings, while a servo unit can be fitted to cars not already so equipped.

CHAPTER 6
bigger engines

Without any doubt, the easiest way of extracting more performance from any of the Ford range of small saloons is to fit them with a bigger engine. This can easily be done, and any engine, from 997 c.c. to 1600 c.c. can be fitted as a direct replacement to any of the Anglia, Capri, Classic or Cortina saloons.

However, there are one or two points to bear in mind when this is being done. To begin with, when fitting, say, a 1500 GT Cortina engine to a 997 Anglia, it is certainly desirable to use the Cortina gearbox as well, and the difficulty is that an all-synchromesh gearbox cannot be mated to a prop-shaft on a car fitted originally, as the Anglia was, with a gearbox with synchro on the top three gears only. The trick here is to use the shorter prop-shaft from the Anglia 1200, which did have an all-synchro box.

The next point concerns the clutch. Diaphragm-spring clutches will not mate to gearboxes designed to operate with earlier coil-spring clutches and in this case the engine, clutch, gerabox complete must be transferred. Otherwise, there's no problem except when it comes to attempting to install the twin-cam Lotus-Cortina engine in an Anglia. This is possible, in so far as it *has* been done,

but involves an immense amount of work and is not really advisable for the amateur.

Push-rod engine installation, however, is really a piece of cake. To do this, you remove the normal engine by unbolting the engine mountings, remove the radiator, take out the engine bell-housing bolts, remove the starter and the clutch slave cylinder. Disconnect all hoses, pipes and wires, attach a chain hoist to the middle two head bolts and raise the engine just enough to take the weight. Then slide it forward away from the gearbox, twist it as it hangs and hoist away. Put it down tidily in a safe place, draw from stores the 1500 GT motor or whatever and reverse this procedure.

This, really is about all there is to it, with the exception of the cooling system. If the bigger engine is being fitted to an Anglia, the thermostat must be removed from the Anglia cooling system: preferably and alternatively, the cooling fan size should be increased to get more air flowing through. All other engines use a bigger fan than the standard 997 component, while the 1340 c.c. engine has a larger cooling system water capacity than any of the others at $10\frac{3}{4}$ pints. The 997 Anglia has a $10\frac{1}{4}$ pint system, while the 1200s and 1500s have only 9 pints.

Next comes the question of increasing the engine capacity itself. This is a popular move on the 1500 c.c. engines In principle, you can bore out the cylinder bores and fit 85 mm pistons to achieve a capacity of 1650 c.c., an increase of 4 mm. However, by no means ever 1500 block will withstand overboring by this amount, and it is best to obtain a ready-bored one from one of the tuning specialists rather than run the risk of spoiling a few.

Boring the twin-cam Cortina-Lotus engine to 83.5 mm will increase the capacity to 1594 c.c., while the five-bearing 1300 engine introduced in 1967 can, in some cases, be bored to 85 mm to increase the capacity to 1400 c.c.

In all cases where the block is to be over-bored by significant amounts it is important to seek expert advice: manufacturing tolerances mean that all dimensions of all parts of the engine can vary by surprisingly large amounts, and if you happen to have a "thin" casting, substantial increases to the cylinder bore will not be possible.

When performance is being improved by fitting larger engines, or by increasing the capacity of the existing power units (which will give a slight increase in brake horse-power but a very substantial torque improvement) careful attention should be given to the brakes, which will again prove inadequate exactly as they would for tuning in any way. Harder linings, or a conversion to disc front brakes where these are not already fitted, are an essential.

CHAPTER 7
the V4

Towards the end of 1965, Ford introduced a new engine line for the Corsair range, which until that time had been fitted with the four-in-line 1498 c.c. engine of the Cortina etc.

Two engines were announced, the first a 1663 c.c., 76.5 b.h.p. version for the de luxe Corsair and a 1996 c.c. one developing 88 b.h.p. Both are 60-degree conformation engines, with a common bore of 93.6 mm; the difference in capacity is achieved by varying the strike, which is 60.35 mm for the 1.7 and 72.41 for the 2-litre. Total overall length of the complete engine is only 20 ins., compared with 22.5 ins. for the four-in-line 1500. Compression ratio is 9 to 1 on the smaller engine, and 8.9 to 1 on the larger, and both, of course, are cross-flow pattern with bowl-in-piston combustion chambers.

So far as tuning is concerned, the same limitations apply as to the 1600 cross-flow Cortinas, but there is more scope for improvements to the breathing since the standard arrangements are poor.

In fact, Ford recognised this, and on the later 2000E model ,which uses the 2-litre GT engine, a twin-choke Weber carburettor and improved manifolding were employed which raised the power output from 88 b.h.p. at 4,750 r.p.m. to 97 b.h.p. at 5,000.

Very little can be done to the heads or combustion chambers. Ports can be polished, of course, and carefully matched to the manifolding: a few tuning specialists have produced improved manifolding for these engines, but generally they have not aroused much excitement in the business. A wider-timing camshaft would improve flexibility, but the only real way of obtaining a substantial power increase is by supercharging: anyone who has looked under the bonnet of a V4 Corsair will immediately realise that the biggest snag here is to find somewhere to put the blower, but if this can be done then power outputs of up to 140 b.h.p. are possible: the engine is extremely well-cooled and overheating would be unlikely to be a serious problem.

Good results have also been obtained from the a weir-type carburettor, such as the Reece-Fish or the Minnow.

Suspension and brakes can be regarded as being identical so far as modification is concerned to those of the Cortina range, while the transmission includes the latest-pattern gearbox with well-spaced ratios, which we have already mentioned.

CHAPTER 8
the twin cam

This engine is, of course, the one fitted to the Lotus-Cortina, Twin-Cam Cortina and, come to that, the Twin-Cam Escort as well. Designated the 125E, it first saw the light as day as far as production cars are concerned in January, 1963. It uses the 1500 engine block with capacity increased to 1588 c.c. by enlarging the bores to 82.55 mm. The top end, of course, is completely different, with a special aluminium alloy head with hemispherical combustion chambers, two rows of valves at an included angle of 54 degrees and twin overhead camshafts, each running in four bearings and driven by a roller-chain of the same pitch as the normal 1500 timing chain. After passing round the crankshaft sprocket, this goes outside the standard camshaft sprocket, inside round an adjustable jockey, outside the two camshaft sprocket once again. The jockey sprocket is spring-loaded and is also adjustable from outside the chain-case; on the driving side, there is a rubber-faced slipper, controlling chain whip. The standard camshaft is retained to drive the distributor and oil-pump, and the crankshaft has extra counter-balance weights, the crankcase being relieved to

make room. As originally announced, this engine produced 105 b.h.p. at 5,500 r.p.m., and was mated to a gearbox with a very high bottom gear and close-spaced ratios; subsequently different camshafts, known as "special equipment" and previously available to special order, were standardised and, with rejetted carburettors (twin 40 DCOEs, of course), power was increased to 115 b.h.p.

The camshafts operate the valves through inverted plunger tappets with shim adjustment, and the plugs are more of less central on the head's horizontal axis and emerge to left or right of the valves on alternate bores. Standard compression ratio with flat-top pistons is 9·5 to 1.

It isn't difficult at all to increase the power of this engine. The first and most basic mod is to take off the head and remove all the burrs, and polish the passages—do NOT open them up in size, though. Simply doing this has given up to another eight horsepower, and apart from this it will run a lot more sweetly. You can take 40 thou. off the head as well, and by fitting the Lotus "special equipment" cams and

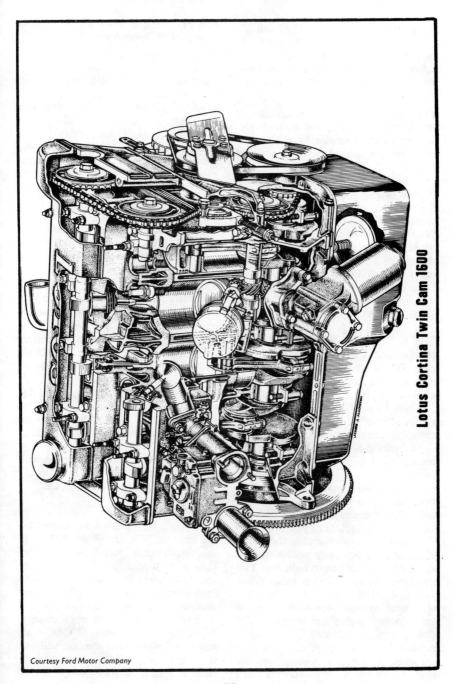

Lotus Cortina Twin Cam 1600

Courtesy Ford Motor Company

carburettor jets and chokes you can get a further increase of ten b.h.p. It already has a good exhaust system, big valves and Weber carbs and for road use there isn't much more you can do.

The main thing about the engine is that the camshaft timing, valve clearances and timing chain tension have a marked effect on the general performance and running of the car. A considerable amount of care and attention should be paid to these points when re-assembling the engine, and the manufacturer's settings should be strictly adhered to. With the engine cold, the clearance between the valve stem and the plunger should be 0·005 to 0·006 in. on the inlets, and 0·006 to 0·007 in. on the exhaust valves. To check the clearances, whip off the cam-cover and, on the valve to be checked, turn the cam until its lobe is exactly opposite the tappet and then put a feeler gauge between the plunger and the back of the cam. If everything is correct all you have to do is to put the cam-cover back on, with a new gasket but if adjustment is needed you will have to remove the camshaft and re-shim the clearance. You get the camshaft out by slackening the camshaft bearing-cap bolts, removing the centre bolt retaining the sprocket and then remove the sprocket altogether from the dowel which holds it in. You can then remove the shaft and withdraw the plungers with a suction-cup valve grinding tool. Now you can get to the shims, and to increase the valve clearance you obviously need a thinner shim, or a thicker one to reduce it. You must use only one shim per valve. When you re-assemble the engine, the camshaft bearing caps must go back on the same journals—they are numbered for this purpose—and should be finally tightened to a torque of 12 lb. ft. The sprocket is properly located on the shaft by means of the dowel and when

you put the bolt back tighten it to a torque of 23–30 lb. ft.

The proper tension of the timing chain should allow a total up-and-down movement of half-an-inch half way between the two camshaft sprockets on the chain's horizontal run. It is vital that the chain isn't over-tensioned—if it is then the ends of the camshaft will probably break off. You can adjust the tension if it needs it by the manual external adjuster, which is a slotted screw with a lock-nut mounted on the offside of the chain cover, just in front of the distributor.

Close inspection of the valve stem-to-guide fit should be made, and if this is over the specified tolerance (0·0018—0·003 in.) then new guides ought to be fitted.

It is surprising how much improvement can be made to this engine by careful assembly. The next step would be to fit the wider-timing camshafts, such as the Cosworth L2. These, combined with the "special equipment" chokes and jets, will give up to 130 b.h.p. And that is about all you can do for road use. Modifications beyond this point would frankly be undesirable on the road because of the loss of tractability which, apart from being unpleasant in itself, would combine with the high gearing on the car to mean too much hard work for the clutch, etc.

Competition tuning

Once again the field is a bit limited for the amateur. You can obtain 140 b.h.p. or so quite simply, with little more work than merely screwing bits on to the standard power unit. But to go above this point is extremely difficult, very expensive and requires facilities and skill probably beyond the amateur's scope. Providing the revs are kept to a maximum of 7,500 r.p.m. you can still use the standard crankshaft, but it will require regular crack testing. Drop-forged steel con-rods are essential—these are available from Cosworth and are in fact longer than the standard ones, so that they bring the piston crowns flush with the block face at t.d.c. and also, of course, effectively raise the compression ratio. With a modified head you can go up to about 11 to 1.

The block can be overbored to give a new bore of 83·5 mm., which will bring the total capacity up to 1,594 c.c., and if the block will stand it—the same difficulties apply on this as on any other Ford block, of course—you can take it out to 85 mm. and bring the engine up to 1,650 c.c. In this latter case, small reliefs will have to be ground in the tops of the pistons to accommodate the valves at full lift.

The head is modified in the same way as for road use—taking off 40 thou and polishing the chambers. The ports can be polished but, once again, should NOT be overbored. You cannot, fit larger valves— it has been done, but this is not an exercise for the amateur any more than casting your own cylinder head would be.

Fit full-race camshafts, such as the Cosworth L1. It will be necessary to counter-bore the cylinder head valve-spring seats to accommodate the extra lift of the cam. To obtain the measurement for counter-boring you must first check the depth of the cylinder head valve-spring pockets, and then counter-bore to the required depth. The important thing is not to counterbore more than is necessary, because this can weaken the platform and might result in the spring being pushed through the head.

Larger jets will be necessary in the carburettors—130 main jets, with 160 air correction jets and 35 pump jets, 45 F9 slow-running jets, 200 needle valves and F16 emulsion tubes, plus the "special-equipment" 33 mm. chokes.

The ignition timing will probably have to be advanced a few degrees, too.

When you are fitting the new camshafts it will be necessary to time them according to the manufacturers' specification, and to do this you will need a supply of off-set dowel pins for relocating the camshaft relative to the sprocket—you will be able to get these from the people who supply the cam.

These modifications, plus careful assembly which, as we said before, shows remarkably high dividends anyway on the twin-cam engine, should give you a racing engine producing between 140–145 b.h.p. As you can see, it doesn't involve much work apart from fitting certain new components, but to get more power than this is a question of re-designing the whole engine, which isn't really the sort of thing you can tackle in the average home workshop.

Suspension, brakes, etc.

Early Lotus-Cortinas were fitted with a special coil-spring/"A" bracket rear suspension set-up which, while undoubtedly giving outstanding good road-holding, proved unreliable in hard use. In 1965, therefore, the system was scrapped and replaced by conventional semi-elliptic leaf springs. Most surviving early cars have probably been converted by now, since several firms specialised in the job: if not, to have the conversion carried out is desirable, as an early car with improved performance will very quickly suffer from trouble in this respect. Ford tuning specialists can undertake the work, and once it has been done the rear suspension can be treated exactly as that of a Cortina GT.

At the front, the Lotus is already lowered and fitted with a special spring strut, and the only thing you can do from which the car would benefit for road use is to fit dampers with slightly firmer settings.

Much the same is true of the car when it comes to setting up the suspension for competition work. Racing-setting dampers, bigger wheels and racing tyres, and the replacement of the rubber anti-roll bar bushes with positively-locating hard metal bearings sums it up. The only necessary improvement to the adequate disc/drum brake set-up is the fitting of harder pads and linings.

CHAPTER 9
body & interior

There is nothing that needs to be done to the bodywork on a car which has been built for road use. Even with the Lotus-Cortina wide-rimmed wheels and fat tyres there is no need even to modify the wheel-arches. About the only mods you need make, if these can really be considered under the heading of bodywork, is the fitting of such extra instruments as you might like to have—on a tuned car a rev-counter is pretty desirable, and an oil-pressure gauge has its uses, too. On rally cars, fitted with a lot of extra lights and electrical equipment, some drivers like to have an ammeter. Most Fords already have water temperature gauges.

Seating, too, is very much a matter of personal taste. It seems reasonable to suppose that if a bloke isn't satisfied with the standard car's performance and has gone to all this trouble to improve, he probably won't think much of the standard seats either. There's all manner of solutions here—a wide selection of special seats is on the market, and you can get special covers which slip over the standard seat and provide it with sufficient extra padding to make it into a sort of bucket seat, offering much-improved support.

When it comes to building a competition car there's a good deal more scope for alterations, and worthwhile ones at that. To begin with, the body can be considerably lightened by replacing all the non-stressed panels—bonnet, boot and all the doors—with glassfibre. You can take out all the glass except for the front screen (this will have to be of the laminated type if it isn't already, because the toughened-glass screen is not allowed in racing) and replaced by Perspex. This must be of at least $\frac{1}{16}$ in. in thickness, and you need to remember that the driver's window has to be openable—at least, you must have some means of getting your arm out to give a signal. Well, that's regulations. Once you've got the Perspex in, treat it as carefully as you can—it scratches very easily, and wiping off the mud-splashes can make scores which stop you seeing out of it as much as the mud did.

Further weight can be saved by removing all the unnecessary accessories and the trim—you can take out the heater, the carpets, remove the bumpers and so on. Before you go stripping the thing down wholesale, though, study the regulations carefully to make sure of the bits that must be left on. This will depend very much on the kind of racing you are doing, of course.

It is definitely not advisable to carry out lightening mods which weaken the shell of the car in any way, and this applies to all the bits which don't open. We rely very much on the rigidity of the hull for the car's roadholding, and you can undo all your suspension work by drilling holes in careless places. If you don't want to go to the expense of glassfibre replacement panels, you can save a useful amount of weight by stripping out the strengthening webs in doors and boot-lid, which won't matter very much on a racing car and which amount to a small amount of surplus weight when you add it all up. Unfortunately this makes them very flimsy and isn't particularly safe so don't do this to the driver's door, not to the passenger's door if passengers are going to be carried. You will also be amazed at the weight of the glass, and you should certainly take out the winder mechanism.

When fitting the driver's seat in a racing car it is the wisest plan to think about it carefully, and to treat it as more important than just a last-minute job to get the thing finished. The seat itself should have a tubular-steel construction, preferably with a p.v.c. covering supported by rubber. The seat frame should be bolted solidly to the floor—the adjustable runners are among those items you can throw away in the weight-saving process, because once you've got the seat on the right position you won't want to move it again, and it is important that it should be rigidly mounted.

For racing, the seat belt should be of full-harness type, with the anchorage points for the shoulder straps fixed in the floor pan under the rear seat, and the lap-strap anchorage located behind the driver's seat. All these anchorages should have a plate at least $\frac{1}{4}$ in. thick under the floor, covering an area round the anchorage of at least 4 sq. in.

Any roll-cage you fit ought to cover the front of the car and provide additional support for the screen pillars, quite apart from what it does at the back. If you look at any rolled-over car you'll see that it is invariably the front part of the roof which has caved in when the screen-pillars have buckled, and this is the bit under which you are sitting, strapped in!

So far as instruments are concerned, the only ones you need for racing are water temperature and oil pressure gauges, and a rev-counter. If this latter item is of the electric variety then you should have it checked for accuracy before you use it and certainly before you rely on it—some of the variations can be surprisingly large.

Nothing much can be done to the steering, apart from fitting a different steering wheel of a pattern to suit your preference, which is usually a smaller diameter one. By the time the suspension has been modified along the lines suggested earlier, the standard steering set-up works out about right more or less automatically. When you do fit the steering wheel, make sure it is of a type known to have a substantial frame work—collapse of the wheel at racing speeds can be very serious indeed, and it has happened.

THE
PERFORMANCE
PAPERBACKS

A NEW SERIES
of
**AUTO ENGINEERING
REFERENCE BOOKS**

The following pages present to you some of the
current SpeedSport and Interauto books for the
motoring enthusiast, the automobile technician
and the motorist.

If you have enjoyed this book you will find the two titles below of interest—from the Speedsport Motobook Range

THE THEORY & PRACTICE OF CYLINDER HEAD MODIFICATION
David Vizard

Profusely illustrated £1.50

The definitive work for the professional but easily read by the novice.

Its contents include.
Workshop equipment, Valves, Guides and Seats, Matching of Ports to Manifolds. CR Calculation. Chamber Reshaping/Balancing methods. Port Design. Combustion Chamber Design. Optimum Valves, springs and plugs — plus specific details on most popular engines and actual size chamber modification templates.

THE THEORY & PRACTICE OF HIGH SPEED DRIVING
Walter Honegger

English version by Charles Meisl

Hard-back bound. Profusely illustrated £1.50

A new book that demonstrates practically how the technique of your driving can be improved. All drivers can use this book to obtain higher average speeds and greater safety. Devoid of long winded theoretical debates, this is a handbook from which the racing enthusiast or road driver will derive immediate benefit.

The author is chief instructor and co-organiser of the Swiss International Racing Drivers Course.

Motorsport

HOW TO START MOTOR RACING. Wally Hall. 011.9. £1.00

The author has had considerable club racing success and has passed on most of the vast experience he has gained. Ideal for anyone at all interested in beginning.

HOW TO START RALLYING. Colin Malkin. 024.0. £1.00

This famous rally driver takes the reader through all the mystiques of rally preparation. Car selection, suitability and setting up. Bodywork, lights, driving and navigation are some of the subjects dealt with. Colin co-drove the winning London to Sydney Marathon car.

HOW TO START AUTOCROSS AND RALLYCROSS. Peter Noad. 033.X. 80p

Like the rest of the 'How to Start' series but for the increasingly popular sport of autocross/rallycross. Like the other authors Peter Noad is an experienced and successful campaigner.

TOUCH WOOD. Duncan Hamilton. 042.9. £1.50

Paperback   25 b/w illustrations

We feel that we have found a great book in **TOUCH WOOD** and have re-issued it as the first title in our reprint series of motor racing classics. Duncan Hamilton was typical of the enthusiastic amateur who went racing for the sheer hell of it. He drove many makes of car to their limit, mostly Jaguars, utterly indifferent to his own safety and surviving many spectacular accidents. He won Le Mans at over 100 mph suffering from a monumental hangover, crashed an aeroplane, was torpedoed twice and helped to put England back on the motor racing map. His autobiography is a marvellous colourful story and has been out of print for a long time.

HOW TO START PRODUCTION MOTOR CYCLE RACING Ray Knight 030.5 £1.00
Ray Knight
Ray Knight is a journalist with 10 years racing, a TT win and lap record to his credit. He passes all his experience to the enthusiast. 'A good guide to success.'

THE *BARRY LEE* BOOK OF HOT ROD RACING   062.3   £1.00

Barry Lee revolutionised Hot Rod Racing in 1970 and in 1971 became British Champion, as well as making successful forays to Denmark and South Africa. In his book Barry Lee shows how he built his Escort, what it's like in a hot rod race, where and when hot rod racing takes place - in fact he writes about everything that an intending competitor, a hot rod fan or spectator will want to know.

Marque tuning guides

TUNING THE MINI. Clive Trickey   001.0. £1.00
The Mini Tuners' Bible; universally recognised as the most authoritative book on the subject. The most popular marque tuning book to be published.

MORE MINI TUNING. Clive Trickey   000.3. £1.00
New! The second edition of the companion volume to 'Tuning the Mini'. Updated with much more information on valve gear, carbs, camshafts and gearboxes.

TUNING STANDARD TRIUMPHS up to 1300cc.   012.7. 50p
Richard Hudson-Evans
Essential reading for Herald, Spitfire, 1300, Standard 8 and 10 owners. Full tuning information.

TUNING STANDARD TRIUMPHS over 1300cc.   029.1. £1.60p
David Vizard
The tuning stages for Vitesses, GT6, TRs and all 2000 units from stage 1 to full race.

TUNING VOLKSWAGENS. Peter Noad   026.7. £1.00
An expert guide to the race and rally preparations of VWs; it covers the various types of car and their development and competition history. Includes a section on Beach Buggies.

TUNING ESCORTS AND CAPRIS. David Vizard   009.7. £1.00
The technical editor of **'Cars and Car Conversions'** explains engine and chassis tuning procedures for both road and track.

TUNING ANGLIAS AND CORTINAS.   003.8 80p
This bestseller deals with engine and chassis tuning and details the early Classic and Capri, the V4 and Twin Cam power units.

TUNING TWIN CAM FORDS. David Vizard   007.0. £1.00
The stage-by-stage modifications for these engines, from 'warm' 1600s to full-race 1800s. Fully illustrated.

TUNING FOUR CYLINDER FORDS. Paul Davies.   059.3. £1.00.
A new edition of this very popular tuning bible for all four cylinder models from Anglia to Cortina MK III.

TUNING BMC SPORTS CARS. Mike Garton   004.6. 80p
The author, once a technical expert at British Leyland Special Tuning Department passes his wealth of experience on to the interested owner.

TUNING IMPS. Willy Griffiths   052.6. 50p
The Imp is one of the most difficult cars to modify. The author lets out all the secrets on what can and cannot be done. **NEW 2nd Edition.**

TUNING VIVAS AND FIRENZAS Blydenstein & Coburn 064.X £1.00
Written by the country's leading experts, this is the first tuning book on these popular cars. It covers all aspects of tuning for both road and track.

TUNING V8 ENGINES. David Vizard   028.3. £1.50p
This book covers the principles involved for modifying a large selection of V8 engines— design trends, supercharging, assembly, part swapping, carburation etc.

TUNING SIDE VALVE FORDS. Bill Cooper   005.4. 80p
This book covers the 100E engine fitted to early Ford Anglias and Prefects now finding their way into many youthful hands.

BUILDING AND RACING AN 850 MINI. Clive Trickey.   010.1. £1.00
Another winner from Clive Trickey who describes here the story of his own racing success in a step-by-step method that can be followed by the would-be racer.

Carburetter guides

TUNING SU CARBURETTERS. 017.8. 104 pages, 30 illus.   70p

The SU carburetter is fitted to all BLMC and many other cars and is often used for carburetter conversions to tuned cars. This book is a complete guide to their tuning, servicing and fitting, with recommended jets and full needle charts, both for the enthusiast and economy-minded motorist. Recommended by the Manufacturer. Covers carburetters fitted to Aston Martin, BLMC, Citroen, Daimler, Ford Conversions, Hillman Conversions, Jaguar, Jensen, MG, Renault, Rover, Triumph, Volvo, also suitable for HITACHI carburetters.

WEBER CARBURETTERS. Vol.1 - Theory & Conversion Practice. John Passini. 018.6.   70p

This book covers the setting-up, method of operation and servicing on one of the finest carburetters available for high performance engines. Written by an acknowledged specialist on these carbs. Suitable in conjunction with Vol.2 for Mini, Ford, Volvo, VW's, Alfa Romeo, BMW, MG, Fiat,Simca, Peugeot and Lancia models.

TUNING STROMBERG CARBU-RETTERS. 006.2.   70p

A similar volume to the SU carburetter book but for tuning the very popular Stromberg carburetter. Again recommended by the Manufacturer. Suitable for Aston Martin, Ford, Hillman, Humber, Jaguar, Sunbeam Triumph, Vauxhall.

WEBER CARBURETTERS Vol.2 - Tuning and Maintenance John Passini   060.7   70p

This is the companion volume to the very successful Weber Carbs book by the same author, which dealt with the Theory of how Webers worked and functioned only. John Passini has worked very closely with the factory to provide in this book all there is to know about Weber tuning and maintenance. Profusely illustrated and complete with needle, settings and application data tables.

**TUNING SOLEX CARBURETTERS R.C. Pack   069.0
                                                                      70p**

This book deals with problems and major tuning characteristics of Solex carburetters, and shows how to obtain maximum power from the engine.

TUNING COMPANION SERIES

TUNING LUCAS IGNITION SYSTEMS   063.1   £ 1.00

This book examines each component in the Lucas ignition system and explains how to test and check that it is functioning correctly. Also dealt with are the special procedures and requirements of systems on high performance engines, with setting up instructions, trouble shooting hints and comprehensive data tables.

INTRODUCTION TO TUNING. 002.X. 50p
ENGINES AND TRANSMISSIONS. 013.5. 50p
SUSPENSIONS AND BRAKES. 027.5. 50p

Martyn Watkins has written a basic guide to the tuning and modification of production cars. These three volumes of the **TUNING COMPANION** series are designed to take the beginner through the theory and then the practice stage by stage. They should then lead him into the more detailed work featured in the rest of the Motobook range.

AUTO ELECTRICS.   David Westgate.   014.3.   £ 1.00
A well illustrated and easily readable guide to the car's electrical system. This book should be a standard work as it covers all aspects of this complicated subject from batteries to ammeters.

CAR CUSTOMISING.   Paul Cockburn.   031.3.   90p
A new book on this increasingly popular form of car modification. Paul Cockburn a brilliant young designer explains the ground work and suggests many practical ideas.

MODIFYING PRODUCTION CYLINDER HEADS.
Clive Trickey.   008.9.   50p
Clive Trickey's famous basic guide to the modification of cylinder heads for improved performance. A standard work which has become a best seller.

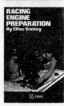

RACING ENGINE PREPARATION.   Clive Trickey.   015.1.   £ 1.00
Fully describes the conversion of mass-produced engines to full blown racing units.

New edition
Castrol Book of Car Care

SBN 902-587-005
This is the new edition of the ever popular Castrol Book of Car Care in a new format and at a new price.
'Car Care' has been rewritten and considerably updated, with new drawings, diagrams and photographs. It now has a full-colour cover.
'Car Care' does exactly what its title suggests under the following chapter headings:
1. A Happy Partnership? 2. Servicing; 3. Bodywork; 4. Engine; 5. Transmission; 6. Brakes; 7. Suspension and Steering; 8. Tyres; 9. Electrics; 10. Breakdown Trouble-shooter; 11. Safety and Security; 12. Castrol at your Service.

25p

Castrol Book of Motor Cycle Care

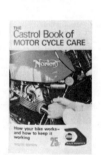

a sister publication to the **'Castrol Book of Car Care'** describes the various parts of the machine tells what they are designed to do and suggests the best course of action for looking after them. Used intelligently it can save a lot of time, money and frustration.

Still very popular and a constant best seller.

25p

The Big Drive

**THE BIG DRIVE.
Richard Hudson-Evans and Graham Robson.
032.1. 50p**
The Book of the World Cup Rally, 1970.
The first behind-the-wheel view of the toughest rally ever—the car breaking London to Mexico Race.

**HOW TO KEEP YOUR VW ALIVE. John Muir. £2.50
'A manual of step by step procedures for the complete idiot'
Softback, ring-bound, profusely illustrated**

This brilliant book has been a huge success in America. It is written by an expert engineer who appreciates that complex technical procedures cannot be followed by the amateur mechanic. He explains how to look after a VW in simple language combined with a wry humour.
Basically a manual, but very different from any others. Extremely valuable even though unusual in approach. It is proving that the success in America was no flash in the pan.

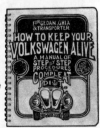

SPEED SPORT AEROBOOKS

For the Aviation Enthusiast

Hot Air Ballooning

Would you like to fly in my beautiful balloon? This catchy little tune must often have passed through people's minds as they stood and watched one of the beautiful modern Montgolfier's sailing through the air above their heads. Hot air ballooning is the oldest form of flight known to man, and is currently enjoying a tremendous renaissance. Since, however, this is such a 'new' aerial sport many potential balloonists find themselves unable to find out enough about it. This book will show the how, the why, and the wherefore of joining-in, helping, buying, and flying one of these lighter-than-air machines. Because ballooning is basically so simple, it is a reasonably easy matter to set out a pattern, which if followed, will lead the novice from stage to stage until he, or she, can become the owner-cum-pilot of one of these magnificent toys.

S.B.N. 85113-036-4   by Christine Turnbull   £1.50

Open Cockpit

In 1930, when he was eighteen years old, the author was granted a short service commission in the Royal Air Force and after completing the then one year's flying and ground subjects training he was posted to the famous 25(F) Squadron at Hawkinge. It was here, except for a few months in the Fleet Air Arm, that he spent the remainder of his five year commission flying Siskins and Furies, both single-seater fighters. After completing a Central Flying School course he joined the De Havilland School of Flying as an instructor in 1935 and of the 120 odd pupils he taught to fly at Hatfield, at least a couple were destined to become famous Battle of Britain pilots.

S.B.N. 85113-040-2   by John Nesbitt-Dufort D.S.O.   £1.00

Scramble

In 1941 he was awarded a DSO and later a Croix de Guerre with silver palm. Due to a certain amount of luck he escaped capture when he crashed in France in 1942 and on return to England was given a test pilot job as an operational 'rest'. He graduated on completion of the very comprehensive course at the Empire Central Flying School in 1944 and finished his second stint in the RAF at the end of 1945 commanding a mixed Spitfire and Mosquito Wing in Norway.

Now forty years since he first soloed and after 10,000 hours flying on 104 types of aircraft, he is more than qualified to discuss some of those planes, putting them into the context of their time and describing their flying peculiarities. In these books he presents a cameo of each aircraft, written in a delightful humourous manner full of personal reminiscence which will fascinate the reader. The books are neat combinations of interesting information and sheer entertainment.

S.B.N. 85113-041-0   by John Nesbitt-Dufort D.S.O.   £1.00

General Motoring

> "I imagine the signs will bring quicker reaction from fellow motorists on a motorway than any amount of gesticulating or pitiful messages written on the back of an envelope."
> **Bradford Telegraph.**

> ".....this could prove to be a big selling line."
> **Auto Accessory International.**

EMERGENCY SIGNS FOR MOTORISTS
ISBN: 0-903192-08-X Size: 11¾ " x 8¼"

A book of easily-recognizable poster-size emergency signs which can save the user time and embarrassment by showing passing motorists that something is wrong. There is a sign appertaining to almost all situations — everything, in fact, from an 'ON TOW' notice to a hazard warning sign. Perhaps of most importance is the inclusion of signs relating directly to accident prevention and the need for medical assistance. A sign such as 'DOCTOR WANTED', displayed with a large cross, attracts immediate attention and is easily understood.

> "Useful when you break down"
> **Sunday Telegraph.**

Officially approved by the Design Centre and featured on the television show "**Drive In**", EMERGENCY SIGNS FOR MOTORISTS provides a service which is long overdue and which, as our roads grow ever more crowded, should become an essential item in the responsible driver's equipment. Remember: It will be worth more than its price when you need it!

> "Quite a bright idea really"
> **'Drive In' Thames Television Motoring Programme**

> "Should be on every motorist's parcel shelf."
> **The Times**

INTERAUTO

Workshop Series

A range of books on important but much-neglected aspects of automotive technology for the engineer and mechanic.

which a P.I. System has been fitted.
With an abundance of clearly laid-out photographs, drawings and plans, and in the same large format as the other titles in the series, this book covers: AE BRICO, BOSCH(Mechanical and Electronic), KUGEL-FISHER, LUCAS & TECALEMIT in relation to the motor vehicles equipped with these systems.

PETROL FUEL INJECT-ION SYSTEMS
ISBN: 0-903192-20-9
Size: 8½" x 11"
380 pages Illustrated

One of the first books published containing detailed information on the construction and operation of most of the major petrol fuel injection systems available today. The opening section deals with the development of the first P.I. Systems, dating as far back as 1940. This is followed by descriptive information and technical data on various systems available on the

The Petrol Fuel Injection Book for Automobiles

Interauto Book Company Limited

present day market.
Finally, service information on a number of vehicles to

ALTERNATOR SERVICE MANUAL
ISBN: 0-903192-28-4
Size: 8½" x 11"
250 pages Illustrated

This valuable publication for automotive electricians deals extensively with the testing and maintenance of Alternators and Regulators. Compiled from genuine manufacturers' service manuals.
CONTENTS: Alternator technology Bosch, Butec, CAV, Chrysler, Delco, Remy, Email, Fiat, Ford, Hitachi, Leece-Neville, Lucas, Mitsubishi.
Motorola & Prestolite
Application tables listing current vehicles and their standard alternators, for easy cross reference.

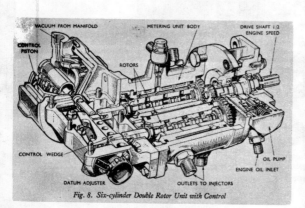

Fig. 8. Six-cylinder Double Rotor Unit with Control

VACUUM FROM MANIFOLD — METERING UNIT BODY — DRIVE SHAFT 1/2 ENGINE SPEED — CONTROL PISTON — ROTORS — CONTROL WEDGE — OIL PUMP — ENGINE OIL INLET — DATUM ADJUSTER — OUTLETS TO INJECTORS

Alternator Service Manual

Interauto Book Company Limited

Automatic
Transmissions
Setting &
Test Data

Interauto Book Company Limited

Crypton
Triangle
(Transervice)
Publications

AUTOMATIC TRANS-
MISSION SETTING AND
TEST DATA
ISBN: 0-903192-29-2
Size: 8½" x 11"
150 pages

Presented in a compact and easy-to-read format are the setting and testing procedures for the more popular automatic transmission systems in their adapted form for use in the majority of vehicles. Additionally, the book contains such information as pressure tables, shift speeds, the location of pressure take-off points, plus comprehensive fault diagnosis charts which enable the user to carry out checks and adjustments with speed and accuracy. The subject of automatic transmission is a complex one. This publication does not purport to be a workshop manual dealing with system overhaul and repair, but it will prove of great value to the service engineer involved in the final on-car setting and testing.

Transmission lists by vehicle make and model as cross-reference.

'Engine and Electrical Service' over 250 pages and 450 illustrations — **£ 2.50**

'Corrective Service' a new approach to fault finding that interprets all oscilloscope traces and meter indications — **£ 2.50**

'Diagnostic Wallchart' 40"x30", for quick reference, it shows all oscilloscope traces and related fault conditions — **£ 2.50**

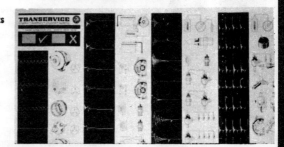

WALL CHART
40" x 30" three colour chart showing all oscilloscope traces. Ideal for checking "fault" conditions.

Interauto Books
for the professional

All priced at **95p**

Interauto Automobile Engineering Reference Series

These books are directed at the car mechanic, the apprentice, the technician and the more experienced do-it-yourself motorist. In clear language, and with numerous illustrations, each title fully details a specific motor engineering subject. All books written by leading motor engineering experts and revised in accordance with 1971/2 technologies.

Part of the series was originally published in Germany by Vogel Verlag, one of that country's largest technical publishers, who have already sold more than 100,000 copies. Licensed editions of the series are also published in Spanish and Dutch.

Each book is designed to be carried around for constant and immediate reference and its handy format facilitates this. Research with major technical booksellers has shown that no reference series of this type has previously been available and that there consequently exists an unlimited demand and sales potential. A further advantage is that the series covers a truly international selection of vehicle systems.

Current titles in this series:

Automobile Fault Diagnosis
Automobile Radio Interference Suppression
Automobile Body & Paintwork Repairs
Automobile Engine Testing
Automobile Performance Testing

Automobile Braking Systems
Bosch Electrical Systems
Caravans - Function, Servicing, Repairs

S.U. Carburetters — Testing, Servicing, Overhauls
Zenith Carburetters — Testing, Servicing, Overhauls
Stromberg Carburetters — Testing, Servicing, Overhauls
Solex Carburetters — Testing, Servicing, Overhauls
Weber Carburetters — Testing, Servicing, Overhauls

(other carburetter books are in preparation)

All your motoring books from ONE source

ALBION SCOTT LIMITED

are the sole distributors of all
SPEEDSPORT and INTERAUTO books.

Albion Scott also distribute a range of
over 1,000 other titles for the motor
vehicle.

We call them all MOTOBOOKS

Motobooks are over 1000 Workshop Manuals,
handbooks, tuning, maintenance and repair
nooks covering practically every car on the
road today. Books on racing, veteran cars,
motor sport, biographies, connoisseur books
and many more

We sell Motobooks

Where ever you see this sign   displayed, i.e. by good bookshops,
motor accessory shops or other retail outlets you can be sure that SpeedSport,
Interauto and the many other Motobooks distributed by us are for sale.

However, if you have difficulties in finding a suitable outlet you may order
directly from us using the form provided in this book.

Nod, Nod, Wink, Wink, Say no more...

These books are for guys like you! Full of pics of the hot ones — by popular demand we include Continental and Oriental models as well as the more usual British types (but no need for phrase books with these little beauties — know what I mean?) Everything from a simple screw to a full strip. Whether you are inexperienced or a pro, you will get more pleasure on the job after reading Motobooks! So don't delay, fill in the coupon below for our catalogue, sent in a plain, sealed envelope.

Please send me your catalogue, I enclose 20p P.O./stamps
I am over 18

Name _____

Address _____

_____

CC2

Albion Scott Ltd., 51 York Rd., Brentford, Middlesex, TW8 OQP.

HOW TO ORDER
Motobooks

Whenever you wish to purchase any of the listed books take this form to your Bookseller or Motorshop who will order the book for you. If this is not possible, mail the order form to us with your payment and we will send the required books to you by return.

Please observe the following instructions:

ORDERING
BOOKS   from
BY MAIL

ALBION SCOTT LTD.·
Bercourt House
51 York Road
Brentford Middx
TW8 OQP England

Identify required books on this form.
Mail complete form to us, with your remittance (either cheque, postal order or cash) to which you must add the postage as set out below.

Make sure that your
NAME and ADDRESS is given in the space below.

Postage and Packing:

		UK	EUROPE	OVERSEAS
Book price to	£2.00	10p	15p	20p
	£3.00	15p	20p	25p
over	£3.00	20p	30p	40p

Dispatch by surface book mail only.

Name ....

Address ....

Special Instructions ....

Get your facts straight from a Motobook

SPECIAL TITLES FROM ALBION SCOTT

Qty.	Title	Price	Total	Qty.	Title	Price	Total
	SPEEDSPORT				**INTERAUTO**		
	Tuning SU Carburetters	70p			Fault Diagnosis	95p	
	Tuning Weber, Vol.1	70p			Interference Suppression	95p	
	Tuning Weber, Vol.2	70p			Body and Paintwork	95p	
	Tuning Stromberg Carbs.	70p			Performance Testing	95p	
	Tuning the Mini	£1.00			Engine Testing	95p	
	More Mini Tuning	£1.00			Braking Systems	95p	
	850 Mini	£1.00			Bosch Electrical Systems	95p	
	Tuning Four Cyl. Fords	£1.00					
	Anglias and Cortinas	80p					
	Tuning Twin Cam Fords	£1.00			SU Carburetters	95p	
	Tuning Side Valve Fords	80p			Solex Carburetters	95p	
	Escorts and Capris	£1.00			Zenith Carburetters	95p	
	Tuning Vivas & Firenzas	£1.00			Stromberg Carburetters	95p	
	Tuning BMC Sports Cars	80p			Weber Carburetters	95p	
	Triumphs to 1300cc	50p					
	Tuning Triumphs over 1300cc	£1.00					
	Tuning the VW	£1.00			Caravans	95p	
	Tuning Imps	50p			Alternator Manual	£2.50	
	Tuning V8 Engines	£1.50			Automatic Transm Data	£2.50	
	How to Start Rallying	£1.00			Petrol Fuel Injection	£3.80	
	Barry Lee Hot Rod	£1.00					
	HS Motor Racing	£1.00					
	How to Start Autocross	£1.00			**CRYPTON**		
	Prod. Motorcy. Racing	£1.00			Engine and Electrical	£2.50	
	Introduction to Tuning	50p			Corrective Service	£2.50	
	Engines and Transm	50p			Diagnostic Wallchart	£2.50	
	Suspensions and Brakes	50p			WORKSHOP MANUALS		
	Auto Electrics	£1.00			quote make, model & year	£2.00	
	Lucas Ignition Systems	£1.00			HANDBOOKS		
	Modif. Prod. Cy Heads	50p			quote make, model & year	75p	
	Racing Engine Prep	£1.00					
	Car Customising	£1.00			Motorist Emerg Signs	75p	
	High Speed Driving	£1.50			Motobook Catalogue	20p	
	Cylinder Head Modific.	£1.50					
	Scramble	£1.00					
	Open Cockpit	£1.00					
	Hot Air Ballooning	£1.50					
	Touch Wood	£1.40					
	Keep Your VW Alive	£2.50					
	The Big Drive	50p					
	Castrol Bk of Car Care	25p					
	Motorcycle Care	25p					
	Qty TOTAL Price				**Qty TOTAL Price**		

NOTES.

Albion Scott Ltd., 51 York Rd., Brentford, Middlesex, TW8 OQP.